PRACTICES
OF
PROSPEROUS
WOMEN

A Spiritual Woman's
Guide to Success

RAVEN MAGWOOD

outskirts
press

WHAT OTHERS ARE SAYING ABOUT *THE 7 PRACTICES OF PROSPEROUS WOMEN*

"I absolutely love *The 7 Practices of Prosperous Women*! Raven provides a soulful and heartfelt read for women of all ages and backgrounds. The words of wisdom and thought-provoking examples she shares will speak to your heart and give you the encouragement you need to not only pursue your goals, but also achieve them. You will laugh and you just may cry. But most importantly, you will walk away with a better sense of self and the confidence to move forward to become all that you dream you can be... And maybe even more!"

-Marla Maples
Humanitarian, Thought Leader, Wellness Advocate,
Award-Winning Singer/Songwriter, Television Personality

"Raven has created an amazing guide for women, which helps us learn how to achieve our dreams and become the best version of ourselves in the process. *The 7 Practices of Prosperous Women* comes at a great time. As women, we need to help create, foster, and empower other women. Social media has warped society into having an unrealistic idea of what being successful or prosperous really is. We need to get back to reality and realize we need to work for what we want. The seven principles implemented in this book will help put you on the right path to success!"

-Alicia Sacramone Quinn
Wife, Mother, 11-Time World &
Olympic Gymnastics Medalist

"From entrepreneurs, to students, to mothers and teens, *The 7 Practices of Prosperous Women* is a MUST READ! If you have a goal, but struggle with self-motivation or getting started, this book will be your new best friend. Raven's detailed description of *The 7 Practices of Prosperous Women* gives the perfect insight for all it takes to become successful in life, no matter what occupation or title you may have. With inspirational quotes and stories, each chapter has a unique yet relatable tone that resonates with many women I know, including myself! This book is a blueprint for any woman who is optimistic about her future, but not quite sure why she has not tapped into her fullest potential."

-Miranda Lattimore
Entrepreneur

"Reading this book is a great blueprint for anyone striving for success and a prosperous life. If there is purpose in your heart and you need a guide to lead you through it, then this book is it. It gives a play-by-play strategy that every woman who desires a prosperous life should follow. It is said that if you want to know the way, ask someone who went before you. This book gives you practical advice on what it takes to see a life of success. What I found to be unique about the subject of prosperity in this book is that there is a clear understanding that prosperity goes beyond just financial gain. Prosperous women are whole and complete in every area of their lives. *The 7 Practices of Prosperous Women* teaches full abundance in joy, self-confidence, authenticity, mental stability, clear direction, and total self-acceptance. Once those are obtained, then the money and your financial explosion are sure to come. This is how you will 'Finish Strong' and enjoy your prosperous life."

-Erica Strong
Author, Transformational Coach, TV Personality

"'Everyone wants to be great'...they just need someone or something to pull that greatness out of them. *The 7 Practices of Prosperous Women* indeed is one of those 'things,' written by one of those 'ones' that will extract that greatness from the reader. Raven has truly laid out practical steps for prospering, illuminated by colorful stories that make it all come alive. Though composed for women, the practices can be applied by men as well. I have been challenged, encouraged, and inspired to continue to push towards becoming and remaining the great version of myself I was created to be."

-Woodrow Dantzler
Principal Owner at DantzlerIII, LLC
Motivational Speaker, Former NFL Athlete

"Raven's book, *The 7 Practices of Prosperous Women*, is very well done! I consider myself to be a strong, hardworking woman. But the minute I started reading this book, I knew I was about to learn something extremely valuable that would help me grow and teach me how to put my priorities in order. Thank you for inspiring me to become a better version of myself!"

-Viviane Brazil
Actress/Producer

"There is so much to say... The mix of faith and practical life application is perfect! I was encouraged, inspired, and motivated to do more! In the busyness of life, sometimes we get covered up in responsibility and forget to dream; it's hard to think and believe big. This book ignites hope, stirs your faith, and gives useful ways to start your journey of pursing the God-given vision for your life. The fact that someone her age has so much wisdom and is so relatable to so many generations is amazing. I can't wait to pass this book along to potential world changers! We need Raven in front of as many young people as possible. Can you imagine what the next generation would look like if they are exposed to this work ethic, passion, and prosperous thinking?!"

-Ashley Bratton
Director of Church Growth & Development,
Coach's Wife, Mom of Three

"I cannot say enough about the powerful messages within each chapter of *The 7 Practices of Prosperous Women*. This book honestly speaks to women in all different walks of life. It teaches us that, as women, we inherently wear many different hats; however, our responsibilities do not have to keep us from achieving our goals. After reading the pages about goal-setting, I cried. I realized that I had let myself become so wrapped up in everyday 'living' that I'd forgotten what my goals were, as well as the little things to help me reach them. Every woman, no matter where she is in life, should read this book!"

-Cilicia Holland
HR Professional

"As a woman in my twenties trying to figure out my purpose in life and the plans God has for me, this book has inspired me to add these practices to my everyday life. This amazing read caused me to reflect on how I am prospering as a woman and how I can leave this Earth in a better place. The tools that Raven provides for us in this book are phenomenal ways that we can take back our minds from negativity, anxiety, and stress. This book can truly help change your outlook on life and I highly recommend this book to ALL women from ALL walks of life. Bravo to Raven! Her gifts and talents are a blessing to everyone."

-Lustra Miller
Dance Educator

"*The 7 Practices of Prosperous Women* is a well-written book that calls out the greatness in any woman, regardless of her age or position in life. This book is an excellent resource that combines lots of practical how-tos along with encouraging examples from others who have experienced success in their own lives. By sharing some of her own personal challenges and victories, author Raven Magwood guides the reader along a path to winning through any circumstance! If there is an area of your life that you'd like to experience victory in, whether it's at work, at school, in your relationships, or personally, let this book be the map that leads you through the steps and see your dreams and goals evolve into reality."

-Kristie J. Wall
Public Speaker and Marriage Mentor

"Sensational! What an amazing book! *The 7 Practices of Prosperous Women* is so inspirational that you will not want to put it down! When I tell you that this book has great nuggets of wisdom for women both young and old, please believe it! I thought I had everything in my life figured out, but this book showed me that I have only scratched the surface! A MUST read!"

-Chandra Magwood
Middle School Teacher, Business Owner

"I've always been a 'Roll With the Punches' type of girl. However, after reading this book, I've embraced the purpose and plans that God has for me in a deeper way. Raven, thank you for not 'sugarcoating' reality and instead candidly opening your life to us. Thank you for showing me how to live life fully and prosperously. *The 7 Practices of Prosperous Women* will revolutionize your vision for your life. It is the perfect weapon in your arsenal for success!"

-Joy Kincade
Gym Manager

"Looking for a guide to self-acceptance? This is it! These steps set a statement about how you should see yourself and your relationship with others. Brilliant!!"

-April Scott
M.Ed., Mother, Teacher, Sister, Friend

"My, my, my... After reading this great read twice, I am ready and rejuvenated to go prosper! Yes, Yes, Yes! Thank you Raven for putting into perspective advice that we should all know and understand as we grow: 'Write the vision and make it plain!' If we write it down, read it daily, and stop procrastinating, we should be successful. With these seven practices, there is no reason we should not be motivated to be phenomenal women and BE PROSPEROUS! Ready! Set! Here we go!"

-Nikki Williams
Co-Owner of NJ Productions, LLC

"This book is remarkable and a true page-turner! I loved it! This read is encouraging and full of wisdom. As I continued to read, I was able to relate to Raven as she shared her personal experiences. I found myself reflecting on my life and taking personal notes. I think this is the perfect read for anyone aspiring to be better than they were yesterday!"

-Kaneesha Kelley
Hair Stylist

"Wow! This is the book I needed in my early 20s when I was still trying to figure out what exactly I wanted to do with my life, my business, and relationships. Actually, I lied! I need this book for RIGHT NOW! Being a business owner, I have struggled a lot with the 'how' of it all so to read this and realize I might be setting my short-term goals too high and getting very discouraged when I don't quickly meet them helps a lot. The part about balancing your life really hit home for me because I lose track sometimes and get so involved in my work that I do not rest, I do not see family, and I barely pay attention to my relationship. This book gives a nice reminder that sometimes I cannot do it all and I just need to rest and spend time with the people who matter. Thank you Raven for such an amazing book! I forget sometimes that you're younger than me lady; I swear you've been here before! You did an awesome job articulating a prosperous woman!"

-Portia Wright
Pastry Chef, Owner of Sweet P's Cakery

"Books change lives, and this one is sure to impact many. *The 7 Practices Of Prosperous Women* is an inspiring book that will encourage you to visualize, focus, claim, and reach your goals. I absolutely love the stories of Raven's personal life challenges and accomplishments, as well as how she uses the seven practices to stay on track each day. Without a doubt, this book is both useful and encouraging. I truly enjoyed the read!"

-Jackie Hagood
CEO of NJ Productions, LLC

"What can I say... Raven has taken all of her life experiences, both positive and negative, and is using those experiences to encourage, motivate, and help us to realize our true mental being. Our mentalities are so critical in the next phases of our lives, which is very important to me since I am only one year away from retirement. I already know this book is going to have a positive impact on my thinking, my behavior, and my attitude! Thank you for sharing these seven practices, which can be applied to your life no matter what age. I'M ENCOURAGED!" #BrainsAndBeauty

-Barbara T. Isom
Savannah River Nuclear Solutions, Nuclear
Operations Support Operator

"*The 7 Practices of Prosperous Women* is timely and relevant for young and seasoned women who desire to succeed and who need more support, tools, and a process for prosperous living. Raven masterfully illustrates the seven practices with vivid examples and compelling life stories that readers may easily understand and apply to their own lives."

-*Dr. Tina Woodard, PHR*
Founder, Speaker, and CEO of I Am BEAUTIFUL,
Inc. and Capstone Performance Solutions, Inc.

"*The 7 Practices of Prosperous Women* is truly an essential source for personal fulfillment and defining one's legacy. These practices will elevate and guide readers to new personal heights and transform many mothers, sisters, and daughters beyond their current struggles and perspectives! Raven is a powerful magnetic source of accomplishment and action. She attracts individuals seeking purpose, fulfillment, and direction on a major scale. Through this book, she makes it her priority to clearly define the road to prosperity and happiness with real-life examples and much more! Her source of personal achievement comes directly from practicing what she preaches! This book is nothing less than mind-blowing!"

-*Justin Oliver*
Editor, Graphic Designer, Founder of J.Vault Designs, LLC

"As soon as I began reading *The 7 Practices of Prosperous Women* I knew that it would be vital to my development as a woman. This book definitely helped me answer questions about my life's purpose. It was as though the universe knew I needed to read this book at this exact moment, during this uncomfortable phase in my life. I thank you, Raven, for writing this book. It is everything that I didn't know I needed!"

-Angel McGowan
College Basketball Head Coach

"Raven's book, *The 7 Practices of Prosperous Women* is like a refreshing drink of ice water on a hot summer day! I was stuck in a daily rut, and this book gave me a renewed sense of self! A much more positive one! My life was controlled chaos at best, and this book gave me the confidence to set new life goals and the courage to go after them! Raven uses personal testimonies, other people's stories, and humor to meet you where you are, no matter what stage of life you are in. *The 7 Practices of Prosperous Women* has so much rich content; you will want to read it again and again. I know I will! Without a doubt, Raven's book will give you the tools you need, as well as the motivation to make the changes you've always wanted to make!"

-Stephanie Epps
Full-Time Mother/Wife, Part-Time Gymnastics Coach

"Raven did a great job laying out *The 7 Practices of Prosperous PEOPLE*, not just Women. I think this book is a great guide and reminder that you can accomplish what you put your mind to, but first you have to know the direction you're trying to go and the vision you're trying to achieve. Raven reminds us that setting short-term goals that line up with the big picture for your life is a must! We must also plan to make time for every section of our lives, making sure we invest in our relationship with God, our families, building our lives, and also having fun. There are so many nuggets! Thanks for sharing your insight and knowledge!"

-Corey Reese
Entrepreneur, Digital Educator

"Wow! *The 7 Practices of Prosperous Women* is truly a phenomenal read for women of all ages, backgrounds, and ethnicities. Even at a young age, Raven has used her experiences and the testimonies of others to create an easy-to-read guide that will give readers the tools they need to succeed in the various aspects of their lives. *The 7 Practices of Prosperous Women* is definitely a book I will be recommending to all of the go-getters in my life!"

-Dr. Nika White
President & CEO, Nika White Consulting

"*The 7 Practices of Prosperous Women* is truly a work of inspiration! What a perfect gift for women, young and old, all around the world. This book speaks life into all who want a brighter tomorrow and gives us a clear example of how to start this journey. I'm so proud of Raven's contributions to help people find their purpose and light in this world. Please pick up this book if you want to see your dreams become a reality!"

-Ruth E. Oliver
Mother, Wife, Sister, Friend, Mentor

"Raven's voice came alive in this book. I found myself reprioritizing both my time and my goals. From my college track days to my current life as a coach and personal trainer, I have always been goal-oriented. As I read, I found myself reliving my years as a collegiate athlete – the pressures, the fears, and the drive to win. Raven truly pinpoints the reality of life as an athlete and directs a clear path to success. Whether in athletics or the real world that awaits after college, this book provides a perspective that can prepare you for both. Overall, *The 7 Practices of Prosperous Women* challenged me to take a look at my God-given purpose and make new goals. It's scary to dream big, but I feel encouraged and empowered to shoot for the moon."

-Sherin Malone
Coach, Personal Trainer

"I am so glad that Raven has written this book for women. These principles are going to help those who read the book and actually do the work accomplish amazing and great things. I love how the book is an easy and exciting read, blessing us with wisdom and knowledge from this young Queen. Raven is giving us tools and strategies to be the best version of ourselves, and I love it. Happy reading."

-Dr. Ja'el The Great
Actress, Speaker, Life Coach, Professor, Absolute Lover of Life

*I dedicate this book to the woman
who is not only my personal hero,
but also my best friend -
my mom, Chandra.*

Table of Contents

Introduction

Going to Prison

I remember the first time I was invited to speak at a youth prison. To be honest, I was a bit scared. I didn't know what to expect, and I wasn't completely sure that the kids would listen to what I had to say. Although the kids were only 13-17 years old, they had committed crimes on a level that I couldn't even imagine. Some of those crimes included armed robbery, attempted murder, manslaughter, kidnapping, and battery.

When I arrived at the facility, I was immediately introduced to the group of twenty youth whom I would be addressing. I was delighted to see that the kids were intrigued by my accomplishments and the fact that I wasn't too much older than they were (I was nineteen at the time). By the time I took the floor, all eyes were on me. And I knew that I couldn't miss the chance to impact these young people's lives.

Shortly after I began giving my testimony, hands started to go up in the air. Already, the youth had questions.

"Raven, when I get out of here, I want to go to college like you did. Was it hard?" one girl asked.

I answered the question, a bit disappointed in myself. I

realized that I had never stopped to think what the kids wanted to accomplish after they finished serving their time. I was so caught up in why they were locked up that I wasn't giving them a chance to explain why they wanted to be free. I directed my next question directly to them.

"What does everyone want to do when you get out of here?" I asked.

This is where the excitement really began.

"I want to be a teacher."

"I want to be a vet."

"I've always wanted to be a music producer."

"A firefighter."

"I really want to be some type of doctor."

All I could do was smile. Despite their current situation, every person in that room had something in their hearts that they wanted to accomplish. No one said they wanted to be a dropout. No one said they wanted to be a gangbanger. No one said they wanted to be broke. No one said they wanted to let their parents down. And no one said they wanted to "just get by." Each teenager wanted something better in life than his or her current circumstance.

It was at that moment that I came to a life-changing realization: Everyone wants to be great. Everyone. We all want to live prosperous, fulfilling lives. And we all want to achieve some level of success. Our interpretations of success might be different, but we all want to triumph. We all want to be happy. We. All. Want. To. Prosper.

But what separates those who actually achieve their goals and those who just sit on the sidelines and watch?

PROSPEROUS THINKING

Dictionary.com defines prosperous as an adjective "characterized by success or good fortune; flourishing." Vocabulary.com takes this definition a step further by stating, "The adjective 'prosperous' can describe anything that's experiencing growth and success." In other words, to prosper is to succeed. But truly prosperous people don't just achieve one level of success in their lives; they continue to grow each and every day to reach their full potential in every aspect of their being. They expand mentally, physically, emotionally, and spiritually, utilizing all of life's experiences to their advantage.

How exciting would it be to wake up each day knowing you are better than you were yesterday? How much joy would you have if all of your relationships were constantly experiencing positive growth? How would you act if you knew that every minute was bringing you closer to achieving your next dream?

If you think this sounds too good to be true, think again. It is totally possible to experience prosperity in each compartment of your life, whether it's a relationship, a career path, a philanthropic endeavor, or a spiritual awakening. But you can't sit on your butt and wait for good things to happen to you. In all honesty, if that's your true philosophy in life, then maybe you should put this book down.

Be real. If making a million dollars were easy, everyone would be a millionaire. If having the perfect relationship were a breeze, no one would get divorced. If walking with God were simple, no one would ever question their faith. And if raising kids was just "common sense," I would never have found myself in that youth prison so many years ago. I want to be clear.

I am not here to sugarcoat anything, or to just temporarily inspire you. My ultimate goal through this book is to give you the tools you need to live the best days of your life for the rest of your life. But, of course, it will be up to you to put in the work and reap the benefits of your efforts.

FINDING THE RIGHT STEPS

Let's just face it. We're women. So we are often required to wear many hats: Mother. Wife. Daughter. Sister. Businesswoman. Homemaker. Teacher. Role Model. Mentor. Nurturer. Spiritual Leader. The list goes on and on. And to top it all off, what makes the job of a woman even more pressure-filled is the fact that we are expected to look good while doing it!

It's hard enough being a woman. Period. But what's harder than that is actually being successful at it. No matter where we are in our lives, we are all striving to achieve some type of success. We all want to reach that next level of greatness. We all want to exceed even our own expectations. However, it is important to never assume that we all want the same things. Because we don't. Each of us has a different definition of success. Each of us wants something different out of life.

What you might want out of life may be very different than what your sister wants, or what your mom wants, or what your neighbor wants, or what I want. And that's okay! All of us are unique, and we should never waste time trying to live someone else's life. What we do have in common, however, is that we all want *something*. We all want to be great. We all want to leave our mark on the world.

So, how do we accomplish that? How do we reach our full potential in each area of our lives? How do we maintain our faith even when times get hard? How do we use the tools God has given us to truly achieve our definition of prosperity? And how do we become successful while meeting all of the constant demands of being a woman? I'll tell you how: *The 7 Practices.*

If you would like to...

- Manage your busy schedule
- Find true happiness
- Think positively
- Make great decisions
- Grow in your faith
- Consistently achieve your goals
- Maximize your earnings
- Improve your interpersonal relationships
- Become the best version of yourself

... then check out the *7 Practices* below, outlined with a brief description.

- **Visualize the End Result**
  Set goals, and own them!
- **Bring the House Down**
  Give your all. All the time.
- **Recognize Your True Strength**
  Realize that your mind is a powerful tool.
- **Use a Time-Out**
  Take time to prioritize your tasks and take care of yourself.

- **Cut Your Losses**
  Remove yourself from negative people and situations.
- **Go Back to Square One**
  Learn from failure, and start anew.
- **Never Throw in the Towel**
  Never, ever, ever give up.

Seems simple enough, right? On the surface, it may appear that way; however, in order to reach your full potential, you must master each and every one of these *7 Practices*, and you must use them in conjunction with one another. Think of the practices working together like a recipe; the result just won't be the same if you leave out one or two of the ingredients.

Like I told you before, I'm not going to sugarcoat this formula. Yes, it will take some work. And yes, you may periodically find yourself outside of your comfort zone. But guess what? Growth only occurs outside of your comfort zone. And prosperous women continue to grow each and every day. If you want what you've always gotten, then continue to do what you've always done. But if you want the opportunity to unlock your full potential in all areas of your life, then turn the page and let's get started!

VISUALIZE THE END RESULT
(Set goals, and own them!)

Imagine you are given a choice to complete one of two jigsaw puzzles. Both puzzles are exactly the same except for one major difference. One of the boxes comes with a picture of the final result, and the other one does not. Keeping in mind that you only have a limited time to finish your choice of the two puzzles, which one would you choose to complete?

Without thinking twice, you would more than likely choose the puzzle with the picture. But why?

With a picture of how the finished product should look, you can be sure of whether or not you are heading in the right direction. In other words, you have a guide for what actions you need to take in order to properly put the pieces together. On the other hand, without a picture you are imprisoned by the process of trial-and-error; you have absolutely nothing to reference in order to determine your actions.

Life works in this same way. In order to accomplish anything, you have to have a picture in your head of what you want to accomplish. Simply put, you have to set goals. Can you imagine if you lived a life in which you never set goals? You wouldn't have anything to reference to determine whether you were heading in the right direction.

Am I saying that you have to know exactly what you want your life to look like in order to be successful? No! It may take years for you to figure out exactly what it is that you want to do. It is not necessary for you to plan out every little detail of your existence. In fact, that would be unreasonable. Life often throws us curveballs that would be impossible to take into account. What I am saying, however, is that you need to make a decision about the general direction that you want your life to take.

Do you want to positively impact other people's lives? Do you want to earn a graduate degree? Is being a good mom important to you? Would you like to travel the world? Do you want to have a family of your own? What qualities will you look for in a spouse? Do you envision yourself as an entrepreneur? Would you like to be a CEO one day? How do you picture your relationship with God?

When you start to answer questions like these, your actions will change for the better. Why? Because everything you do will begin to line up with the direction you want your life to take. For example, if Grace says she wants to be a doctor, she will make it a point to get good grades so that she can get into a good medical school. She won't slack off academically, because she understands that the achievement of her goal depends on her good grades. The same thing is true for Samantha. Let's say she has a goal of becoming the future governor of her state. Since she is aware that individuals running for office are under constant scrutiny, she will stay out of trouble to prevent her past from ruining her future. In another example, Nicole and her husband find out she is pregnant. Knowing she wants to give birth to a healthy child, she stops drinking her daily glasses of wine and begins to eat a more nutritious diet.

Although the women in the examples above may not have every detail of their lives planned out, they do have an idea of the direction that they want their lives to go. This helps them in making their day-to-day decisions. With no goals, individuals tend to simply walk aimlessly through life, because they have nothing to guide their decisions. It's like driving down the road with nowhere to go. If you don't have a destination in mind, then it really doesn't matter which roads you turn on.

Don't be one of those people who just roam pointlessly through life. Start today and pinpoint the direction you want your life to take. It doesn't matter what you've done up to this point. What matters is that you make the choice to move forward in a direction that will bring you closer to personal prosperity.

If you think it's hard to visualize the end result, trust me, it's not as hard as you think. You do it all the time. You think about what you're going to wear on a date before you actually put your clothes on. You think about which route you're going to take before you hop into your car to travel across town. You think about the ingredients that comprise a meal before you cook it. Now, just take that a step further. Today, decide what direction you want to go as a woman full of passion who is ready to attack her dreams.

Think about it this way. If you don't decide right now what direction you want your life to take, someone else will decide for you. Whether it's a friend, family member, parent, boss, or random person, someone else will always make decisions for you if your personal intentions are not clear.

I remember when I first set foot on my university's campus as a 16-year-old kid. It was the first time I had been away from home, and I was excited to start living the college life. Although I was thrilled to begin life as an "adult," I knew one of the goals that I had set for myself: to graduate from college with a perfect 4.0 GPA. Throughout my schooling, I had never made a B on a report card, and I wanted to keep that straight-A streak going. Because I was so set on keeping a perfect GPA, I let nothing distract me. Yes, I had fun. I cheered my team on at football games, I attended my share of parties, and I hung out regularly with my friends. However, I always knew when to say no, because I was so intent on finishing school with a 4.0. Had I not set that goal (and others) for myself, there would have been nothing to keep me from having TOO much fun.

The same is true in your own life. If you don't know what kind of person you want to be, you will let another person get you in trouble. If you don't set standards for yourself in relationships, you will let anyone treat you any kind of way. If you don't decide to pursue what interests you in life, you will likely end up at a job that you hate. The key is this: You want to make sure that when you look back on the book of your life that it was written with your own pen.

Okay, so now that you realize the importance of setting goals, it's time to start setting them! The first thing that you must understand is that there is a method to setting your goals. If you set them too low, you may never reach your full potential. If you set them too high, you may become discouraged. If you only set short-term goals, you may lose sight of what you ultimately want to accomplish in life. And if you set too many long-term goals, you may forget to live in the present. Oh, and let's not forget what will happen if you set goals that have nothing to do with the things that make you happy in life. At that point, you're just miserable. So, what should you do?

Set short-term goals that relate to your long-term goals. Why? Setting goals in this way will help to keep you motivated. By setting these short-term objectives, you will be able to continually evaluate your progress toward your bigger goals. For example, let's say Sally has a goal to lose ten pounds in the next two months. If she steps on the scale every other day and sees that she has not yet lost the full ten pounds, she could easily become frustrated. On the other hand, she could set a short-term goal to lose one pound in one week by eating nutritiously and exercising. Once she accomplishes that, she can set another goal to lose two pounds in the next week by continuing to eat right and completing a seven-day, intense cardio workout. After achieving that, Sally can then set another short-term goal to lose another pound by running a mile every morning for a specified period of time, while still continuing her healthy diet. If she moves forward in this way, by the end of two months, Sally will have lost those ten (or more) pounds, thereby achieving her goal. She'll get to see the results that she desires by setting and accomplishing smaller goals the whole time she is pursuing her biggest goal.

If I were to tell you to fold a sheet of paper in half and list your short-term goals on the left side and your long-term goals on the right side, I should quickly notice their relation to each other. For every long-term goal that you've set, I should see a short-term goal that directly corresponds to it, letting me know that you're on the right track. That's the purpose of short-term goals. It gives you something tangible to do in the present that will bring you closer to achieving your bigger goals. Keep in mind that you can always set new short-term goals once you accomplish them, but you consistently need something to help you measure your progress toward your bigger goals.

In my own life, I create lists of both my short-term and long-term goals on a regular basis. By doing so, I force myself to stay on track and I am constantly reminded of the personal vision I have built. In fact, during a particular time in my senior year of college, this is what my list of goals looked like:

SHORT TERM (within the next few weeks)	LONG TERM (within the next year or two)
Get As on all of my upcoming exams.	Graduate summa cum laude with a 4.0 GPA from the Calhoun Honors College at Clemson University.
Finish the introduction of my new book.	Publish my third book (*The 7 Practices of Exceptional Student Athletes*).
Write my mom a letter telling her how thankful I am to be her daughter.	Maintain a great relationship with my mom, dad, and brother.
Take my brother to the movies.	
Spend a "father/daughter" day with my dad.	

Read the entire book of Job.	Keep a strong relationship with God.
Give a speech at a school, church, or business.	Speak to audiences of all age groups in different parts of the country.
Look for part-time opportunities that will allow me to develop my leadership skills.	Gain experience working for someone else (in order to become a better leader).
Finish my screenplay.	Make an independent film.

If you notice, every long-term goal that I listed had a short-term goal that would help to keep me on track. With so much going on in my life, sometimes it was hard to stay focused; however, I made a conscious effort to do so. Anytime I accomplished something on my short-term goal list, I would come up with another short-term goal that still corresponded with my long-term goal. Once I accomplished that, I would write down another short-term goal. And another one. And another. By the time I looked back on my life a little over a year later, I realized that I had accomplished every single one of my long-term goals! But that wasn't the end of my journey. After celebrating my milestones, I went right back to the drawing board. I created a new list with updated short-term and long-term goals.

One thing that I want you to recognize about my list of goals above is that not every goal was extremely specific. Yes, I knew I wanted to publish a book, graduate with a 4.0, and keep a strong relationship with God. However, the last long-term goal on my list simply stated, "Gain experience working for someone else." I didn't know exactly what I wanted to do or for whom I wanted to work. I just knew that in order to be an effective leader as an entrepreneur, I needed to understand what it meant to serve another organization.

For months, I stayed on the lookout for a potential job opportunity. Despite my efforts to find a meaningful part-time job, nothing promising came my way. I continued to search and work toward my other goals with the hope that something would work out in the near future. Then, out of the blue, one of my former gymnastics teammates called me about a job opening at a nearby gymnastics facility. The owner was looking for someone knowledgeable of the sport who could help coach the high-level gymnasts.

I immediately reached out to the gym manager and was hired on the spot! Days later, I found myself coaching an amazing group of teenage girls. I was excited to not only be back in the gym, but to also have a positive influence on these girls' lives beyond the sport of gymnastics.

Three years later, I am proud to say that my mom and I became co-owners of that very same gymnastics facility. What started off as an unexpected part-time job opportunity turned into a life-changing and profitable entrepreneurial adventure. I say all of this to emphasize that you don't have to know exactly what you want your life to look like in order to be successful. You just need to know the direction that you want to travel on your life journey. I had no idea I would be coaching a gymnastics team, and I definitely didn't know that I would co-own a gym. However, I did know that I wanted a job opportunity that would give me a chance to serve others and hone my skills as a budding entrepreneur. As it turned out, everything would fall into place to make that dream an amazing reality!

"Every achievement, big or small, begins in your mind." –Mary Kay Ash

Don't set your short-term goals too high. You hear it all the time: "You can do whatever you put your mind to." "The sky is the limit!" "Reach for the stars!" While all of this is true, you must be smart in how exactly you reach for those stars. It is very easy to become discouraged if you set your short-term goals too high. If you're working hard every day, and you can't see progress in achieving your ambitions, you may grow disheartened. For example, let's say you have a long-term goal of being able to run a mile in seven minutes. If you currently take ten minutes to run a mile, don't set a short-term goal to run it in eight minutes. Why? Because you're going to work hard every single day; yet you aren't going to suddenly be able to shave two minutes off of your mile time. And then what happens? You get frustrated.

So what should you do instead? Set a short-term goal to run a mile in nine minutes and thirty seconds. When you accomplish this feat, you will be satisfied and ready to set another goal to reach nine minutes. When you reach that, you can set another goal. Then you can set another one, and another one, until you are able to run a mile in seven minutes.

There's nothing wrong with challenging yourself. In fact, I encourage it. The key is to set your short-term goals high enough to make you work, but low enough that you can reasonably achieve them. Then, as you notice yourself getting closer to achieving your short-term goals, you can make new ones. Continue this cycle and watch as you climb the ladder of success. It works. Trust me.

Don't set your long-term goals too low. If your long-term goals are set too low and you are constantly achieving them with no obstacles, then you aren't challenging yourself enough. Challenges are important because they force you to grow and allow you to reach your full potential. Although some obstacles may be difficult, prosperous women can't move forward in life when things are always easy.

What would happen if you never had challenges? What if you never had a thought-provoking professor, a difficult boss, a family crisis, a demanding coach, a frightening illness, or a relationship setback? If things in life were always easy, you would never know what you are truly capable of.

On this journey, we have to constantly push ourselves to be the best people we can be. We can't place limits on our lives by always doing what's easy. Sometimes we just have to set high goals and work our butts off to achieve them.

Think about how you feel when you accomplish something challenging, whether it's making an A on a difficult exam, getting into law school, birthing a child, receiving a promotion, or overcoming a family issue. At first, you are elated because you achieved a great victory. Then you begin to ask yourself, "How did I do that?" You may even comment, "I don't think I would be able to do that again."

Sometimes we surprise ourselves with how strong we really are. That's why I say to be careful about setting your long-term goals too low. In life, you can't be afraid of a challenge. You can't be afraid of failure. You have to go after what you want, regardless of how difficult it may seem. You were not born to stand on the sidelines and play it safe. You were put on this earth to grow and become the best version of yourself that you can be. But guess what? Growth never occurs inside your comfort zone. You have to be willing to set your goals high and make your dreams come true!

Write it down! A goal that isn't written down is just a wish. Don't allow your goals to exist only as thoughts. Make them tangible and be specific. No matter how good you think your memory is, it is very important that you write down all your goals, both short-term and long-term. When you write them down, you can see what you've written, visualize your accomplishments, and cross out your achievements.

When you write down your goals, it's almost like you've written a contract with yourself. On a tangible sheet of paper (or wherever you choose to write your goals), you can see what direction you want your life to go, both in the short term and the long term. You can see this list every day, and you don't have to worry about forgetting objectives that you have set for yourself. You also have a chance to literally see when you accomplish your goals.

I remember when I had a goal to turn one of my story ideas into a full-length screenplay. Writing a movie script is definitely a daunting task, but I made the goal tangible by formulating my short-term goals into a checklist. It felt so great to put a check mark by each of the smaller goals I accomplished as I worked my way to completing the entire script. As simple as it sounds, having a tangible list of my goals helped me to accomplish my task. After just a couple dedicated months, I was able to place a big check mark by the words, "Finish my screenplay!" I then set another goal: Turn my script into a feature-length independent film. About a year later, I was able to put a check mark by that too. Yes, accomplishing those goals was beyond exciting. But it also gave me a weirdly satisfying feeling to be able to see all of the check marks written on my goal list. In an odd way, the completed checklist made everything real.

"And the Lord answered me: Write the vision; make it plain on tablets, so he may run who reads it." –Habakkuk 2:2

Habakkuk 2:2 states, "And the Lord answered me: Write the vision; make it plain on tablets, so he may run who reads it." Although this is a very popular Bible verse, the true significance of the words is often overlooked. Notice that the sentence doesn't stop with, "Write the vision." The verse continues with, "Make it plain." It is extremely important that when you write down your goals you are not only clear about what you want, but the various steps you will take to get there.

As I said before, you don't have to know exactly what you want in all aspects of your life. But you do need to decide what direction you want your life to take and start taking steps to move in a positive direction. At any given moment, there is something that you want to accomplish, whether it's finishing a business plan, graduating from college, giving a presentation, joining a team, or making a difference. Clearly write down what it is that you want, and write down the steps that you will take to get there. It should be clear enough that if others read it, they could essentially run with it. In other words, anyone reading your goal list should not only be able to comprehend where you want to be in life, but they should also have an idea of what it will take to get there.

I was once talking to a young woman (we'll call her Sarah) about her life goals when she made the following statement: "I just want to be happy."

I replied, "That's great. But could you be more specific about what makes you happy?"

She thought about it for a while and said, "I'm always happy when I'm writing."

"Okay! So, what do you like to write about?"

"I love creating fictional stories."

"Short stories?"

"Yes, but I want to eventually write a book."

"Why did you say, 'eventually?'"

"Um, I don't know," Sarah replied.

"But, you do want to write a book?"

"Yes. Definitely!"

"Well, you've just made a long-term goal! Why not start making short-term goals that can help you accomplish that?"

Sarah immediately filled up with excitement and joy. She now had something she could work toward! I explained to her the importance of writing down this goal and placing it somewhere that she could plainly see it every day.

Sarah could have easily just written down "be happy" on her goal list. In fact, I encourage everyone to make it a point to embrace happiness each and every day. But that general statement wasn't clear. It wasn't plain. It wasn't providing her with the direction she needed to take each morning when she woke up. Because, to be completely honest, she could have been happy doing a myriad of things with both good and bad consequences. The key for her was being specific about what she could do that would continue to bring her joy.

By writing down her short-term and long-term goals, Sarah clearly created a vision of where she wanted to be, and anyone who looked at her goal list would be able to see exactly what she was striving to achieve in her life. So, don't hesitate! Write down your goals. Make them plain. And run with them!

Tell someone. Notice I said tell *someone*, not *everyone*. Whether it's a parent, sibling, friend, cousin, or mentor, there is someone in your life who believes in you. There is someone who holds you accountable and encourages you when times are hard. Tell this person the vision you have for your life. Let them know your goals, both short-term and long-term.

Why is this important? You want this person to serve as a constant reminder of the goals that you have set for yourself. You want them to support you and keep you aware of your goals when you are tempted to give up. That is why it's so important for you to find the *right* person to tell. You can't just go around telling everyone what you want to accomplish in life, because not everyone will believe in the beauty of your dreams. But once you have found the right person (or people), don't be shy about showing them your goal list. Remember Habakkuk 2:2? Your goals should be written so plain that "he may run who reads it." Simply put, your trusted circle of supporters should be able to run with your vision when it's presented to them. Since they are there to support you, they should be able to clearly see your targets and offer support whenever necessary.

When you have succeeded in finding the person with whom you wish to share your goals, you will find that the process of telling them will work to your psychological advantage. How? Well, when you let someone else know the plans you have for yourself, you are more likely to go through with them. This is because, in the back of your mind, you not only want to keep the promise to yourself, but to your supporter as well.

I remember hearing the story of a woman who vowed to quit smoking. Although she had been smoking for most of her life, she made a promise to her daughter that she would quit. As she talked about her journey, she explained the critical role that her daughter played in the process. She said, "Every time I wanted to pick up a cigarette, I remembered the promise I made to her. I just couldn't let her down." Although the process was very difficult, she was proud to say that she eventually won the fight against her addiction. Awesome, right? This is just one of many examples that demonstrate the importance of having someone in your corner who will hold you accountable to your dreams and goals. Who will that person be for you?

NOW IT'S YOUR TURN! In the space on the next page (or on a separate sheet of paper), fill in your short- and long-term goals. Start by filling in the right side first. No matter how big they are, list all of the goals you would like to achieve within the next few years. Then fill in the left side with goals in the short term that will keep you on track in accomplishing your bigger goals. When you're done, show this list to someone you trust who can support you and hold you accountable on your journey to success.

SHORT TERM	LONG TERM

Claim your goal. Now that you have your goals written down, it's time for you to claim them. You have to have faith that whatever you set your sights on is yours, no matter what it may be. Never, ever pursue your goals in doubt. Instead, believe in yourself, more than anything in the world. Yes, there will be people who will doubt your abilities. But you can't doubt yourself. Believe in your capability to accomplish your goals, because if you don't, no one else will.

Claiming your goal doesn't mean to just say, "I can do whatever I set my mind to." And you can't just state, "I'll accomplish that *eventually*." Claiming your goal means you have to put your name on it. You have to feel it. You have to believe it's yours. And then once you believe it's yours, you have to act as though you have already achieved it.

When I say, "Act as though you've already achieved your goals," I don't mean for you to act like you're already a millionaire and go on a crazy shopping spree. Doing that will surely set you up for failure. Acting as if you've already achieved your goals is more about your mindset. In order to get to the next level of your life, you have to have the mindset of the next level. If you want to achieve greatness, you have to think great. If you want to be financially free, you have to let go of a poverty mentality. If you want to be seen as a positive person, you have to stop finding the negative in every situation. If you want to be a CEO, think like a CEO. It's time to dress for the job you want, not for the job you currently have.

As I mentioned before, once you have claimed your goal and are acting as though you have already achieved it, you can't allow anyone to put doubt in your mind. If you've truly claimed your goal, it's yours. Don't let anyone else take it away from you. People may say you're too old, too young, too tall, too short. Some people may say you're not good enough, not smart enough, not experienced enough. Don't listen to them! Haters will hate. It's what they do. But never let a hater put doubt in your mind, because you are destined for greatness!

Visualize. Yes, find a quiet place and visualize! Envision yourself attaining your goals. Imagine the moment you achieve your dreams. Whether it's walking across that graduation stage, finishing your first script, birthing your first baby, obtaining that advanced degree, or starting a successful business, you have to see yourself achieving a goal before it can actually come to pass.

When I say to visualize, I don't mean to just sit on the couch for two seconds and pretend all your dreams have come true. You need to be specific. What exactly have you accomplished? What does it feel like? What is your state of mind? Who is there with you?

If you still have a few semesters left of school and you become discouraged, visualize the end result. Envision yourself walking across the graduation stage, shaking the president's hand, and obtaining your degree. Feel the joy of all your hard work finally paying off in that moment.

If you are preparing for a big sports competition, run through the movements of your body in your head. Place yourself in different scenarios and practice what you would do mentally. After all, multiple brain studies have revealed that thoughts often produce the same neurological patterns as actually performing an act. In one instance, a study looking at brain patterns in weightlifters concluded that the same brain patterns activated when a weightlifter physically lifted hundreds of pounds were also activated when the weightlifter only imagined lifting. Crazy, right?

"Create the highest, grandest vision possible for your life, because you become what you believe." –Oprah Winfrey

As a gymnastics coach, I have been able to see the power of visualization firsthand. I remember a time when one of my girls was having a very hard time in the gym. (Let's name her Megan.) She was scared to perform her skills, and it got to the point at which she was dreading the thought of coming to practice each day. From the outside looking in, it seemed as if her gymnastics career was coming to an end; however, after having a long conversation with her, I realized that she still wanted to do gymnastics. The question then became, "How do we get her to do her stuff?"

I thought about it. I prayed about it. I thought about it some more. Finally, I called her mom to the gym for a meeting.

"I have a suggestion about how to get Megan back on the right track," I began. "You may not agree with it, but I really believe it can work."

"We trust you," she stated with confidence.

"I think she should take at least a month off from gymnastics."

Her mom didn't reply. The team was just starting competition season, and she knew how pivotal it was for the girls to attend every practice (five days and almost twenty hours per week). Taking a month off would be huge. In fact, it could mean the end of her competition season. But I continued.

"I've seen this happen before, and as bad as it seems, I think Megan can really benefit from going home every day after school and visualizing herself doing perfect routines. I don't want her to come to practice, and I don't want her to try to do any gymnastics at home. She just needs a break from the gym, and all I want her to do is imagine where she wants to be. She's having a mental block right now, so if she can replace these negative practice experiences with positive thoughts and visualization, it is highly likely that she can come back even stronger than before."

Although I was confident in my assessment, I realized how crazy I must've sounded to Megan's mom. Did I really just suggest missing an entire month of practice in order to use that time "pretending" to be a great gymnast? Well, yes. Yes I did.

At that point in time, we had tried everything to get Megan more confident in the gym. We tried private lessons. We tried positive reinforcement. We tried negative reinforcement. We allowed more time in the schedule for her to do more skills with which she was comfortable. We literally tried everything, but nothing would work. She didn't want to quit, so this seemed to be the last resort. I gave her a hug and told her that I would see her in a month.

When she came back to the gym, we couldn't go straight into working her harder skills. We had to start with strength and flexibility training, so that she wouldn't get hurt. Even though we were only doing the basics, I could tell that Megan was a different person. When we were finally ready for her to start doing her skills, she was fearless. She no longer hesitated before performing a skill, and she seemed genuinely excited to be in the gym.

After a few days of having great practices, Megan's mom approached me and gave me a hug.

"I just want to say thank you for believing in her."

I replied by saying, "I've always believed in her. But I think this time allowed her the opportunity to start believing in herself."

While visualizing the end result is only one ingredient in the recipe of prosperity, it is a very important one. Megan couldn't move forward in her gymnastics career, because she was allowing her present fear to overtake her mind. That fear contributed to scary falls and bad repetitions, which further reinforced her fear. By removing herself from the physical aspect of gymnastics and allowing herself the time to visualize, she essentially used her mind to recreate a more positive image of the sport she loved. By the time she returned to practice, the negative, fearful thoughts were dissipated, and she was ready to achieve all of her goals! Moving forward, we made it a point to not only concentrate on the physical training, but to also give her time to visualize where she wanted to be. This philosophy has proven to work wonders!

As Megan's story shows, visualization is an important key to success. By taking the time to set goals and creating positive images in your head, you give yourself the unique opportunity to unlock your full potential. I mean, think about it. If you can't use your own mind to picture wild success, how do you expect to actually achieve it?

Create a vision board. How often are you reminded of your goals? Hopefully, multiple times each and every day. The best way to be reminded of your goals is to put them in a visible spot that you visit extremely often. You could create a list of goals that you keep in your wallet. Or you could write your goals on your bathroom mirror. But my personal favorite is to create a vision board that you keep in your bedroom.

What is a vision board, you ask? It's an area in which you put a representation of all your goals. This could consist of pictures, lists, writings, drawings, and much more. Let's say, for instance, you have a goal of making a million dollars. You could write a check to yourself for a million dollars and place it on your board. If you're working hard to obtain a degree, you can put a picture on your board of a mock degree from your college/university. In addition to the pictures and drawings, you can also place your list of short-term and long-term goals on your board. The possibilities are endless.

On my vision board, I have a myriad of things. Pictures of individuals I really want to meet. Copies of checks I want to eventually be able to write (without bouncing them). A complete list of my current long-term goals. Ideas for future books and screenplays that I want to write. Pictures of people with whom I want to be able to work. Quotes that have inspired me. Bible verses I live by. Brands I want to sponsor me. Dresses I want to wear to red carpet events. Organizations I want to impact. Representations of milestones I want to reach. Places I want to travel. And things that I want to be able to buy. It's basically my dream life manifested on my wall.

In addition to my vision board, I have other methods that work to remind me of my goals and the person I want to be. For instance, I sleep with my Bible under my pillow to remind me of my faith. I read biographies about successful people to learn about their journeys. Before I moved from my parents' house, I even took a Sharpie and wrote inspirational quotes all over my bedroom walls to help me keep a positive mentality. (They didn't mind!) Whatever you want to do to supplement your vision board is fine. The point is that you want things around you that will constantly remind you of your goals and keep you in a frame of mind that will allow you to achieve them. When times get hard, you need to have something to keep your spirits lifted and remind you of what you're working toward.

Don't get caught up in the "how." Many people fail to begin working toward their goals because they're not sure of how they're going to achieve them. They know *what* they want, but they don't know *how* they are going to get there. It isn't necessary to plan out every little detail of the path you're going to take to reach a goal, as long as you know what it is that you want and take initial steps to achieve it.

Jack Canfield, co-creator of the *Chicken Soup for the Soul* series, once gave a very thought-provoking analogy that relates to this point: "Think of a car driving through the night. The headlights only go a hundred to two hundred feet forward, and you can make it all the way from California to New York driving through the dark, because all you have to see is the next two hundred feet. And that's how life tends to unfold before us. If we just trust that the next two hundred feet will unfold after that, and the next two hundred feet will unfold after that, your life will keep unfolding. And it will eventually get you to the destination of whatever it is you truly want, because you want it."

Your short-term goals are like the 200 feet you can see with your headlights. As long as you continue to accomplish the short-term goals on your list, you will steadily be making your way to your targeted end, even if there are detours along the way. You don't have to see a detailed plan of the entire journey. But sooner or later, you'll look up and realize you have reached your destination.

Open your eyes. I mean this figuratively. Of course your eyes are open if you're reading this book. What I really mean is "be aware." Don't be stuck in your own bubble. Take the time to understand what it will truly take to achieve the next level of success. Whether you choose to read a book, flip through the pages of an industry magazine, surf the web, or watch a documentary, always make sure you take the time to step outside of yourself and gain insight into the ins and outs of the goals you have set for yourself.

An ancient proverb says, "To know the road ahead, ask those coming back." In other words, do your homework and allow yourself the opportunity to learn from those who have been where you want to be. Apply for internships. Shadow successful professionals. Conduct interviews. Do what you have to do to get the "inside scoop." By doing so, you will have a better understanding of what you're getting yourself into, and you will also be able to decide if you're even willing to put forth that effort.

When I was a little girl, I would often say that I wanted to be a surgeon. Adults told me all my life that I was smart enough to be a doctor and that I would be wasting my intellectual abilities if I didn't go into a challenging field. I internalized those comments, and I found myself daydreaming about my life as a highly-sought-after surgeon. Before long, it was time for me to declare a major and, of course, I went the medical route.

It didn't take long to realize that I was actually good at all of the medical stuff. I aced every class, whether it was biology, advanced chemistry, statistics, you name it. My professors gave me high marks, and my advisor even asked if I wanted to apply to medical school early. After all, I was a 17-year-old junior in college with a 4.0 GPA. "You'll have no trouble getting into the medical school of your choice," my advisor stated with confidence. Too bad I was about to break his heart.

As I started thinking more about my future, I began doing more research. I watched documentaries on surgeons; I talked to surgeons; I Googled "day in the life of a surgeon." I also tried to watch the recordings of a few surgical procedures (notice I said "tried").

The more research I did, the more I realized that I wasn't as passionate about medicine as I thought. While I was good at all of the textbook material, the life of a surgeon didn't particularly appeal to me. First, I've always enjoyed being able to set my own schedule. Whether I want to work at one o'clock in the morning or in the afternoon, I've always enjoyed being able to make that determination. As a surgeon, I would often be subject to someone else's schedule, particularly in emergency situations. And let's face it; emergencies don't tend to happen at convenient times. Second, I realized how often I would literally have someone else's life in my hands. Let me be honest. I cried on and off for two days when I ran over a squirrel. I couldn't even begin to imagine if someone died on my operating table. Third, there's the issue of blood. I'm not the biggest fan of it. And surgeons see a lot of it. Seemed a little bit like oil and water to me. Then there's the whole school thing. I would have to spend many more years at an educational institution, amassing a large amount of debt, learning difficult concepts about something that I wasn't even sure I wanted to pursue.

Would I really be willing to put forth the amount of effort required to become a surgeon when I wasn't truly in love with the idea in the first place? Then my mom asked me a question.

"Rae-Rae, why do you want to go into medicine?"

"Because I can help people. And the money isn't too bad either," I replied.

"That's not the right answer," she said immediately. "*Why* do you want to be a doctor?"

At that point, I realized that the only reason why I ever formally pursued medicine was because that's what everyone else expected me to do. However, after seeing what it actually took to be a surgeon, I didn't want to do it, whether I was capable of doing it well or not. My mom continued with another question.

"What would you do if someone would pay you any amount of money to do it?"

Without hesitation, I said, "I would speak and write so that I can inspire people."

"Then that's what you should do."

The following Monday I went to see my academic advisor to change my major to Communication Studies. At first, I was scared of what other people would think. But soon after taking my first Communications class, I knew I had made the right decision. Each class inspired me, and work just never seemed to feel like work.

No matter what your goals are, always make sure to open your eyes to what it will really take to achieve success in your field. Any feat takes hard work, but are you willing to put forth that effort? Do you love what you're doing so much that you can grind through pain and smile through adversity?

Trust me. On your journey to success, you will face many obstacles. But you should be so passionate about your goal that those difficulties don't even stand a chance of throwing you off course. Having ambition is one thing. Being realistic is another. If you've never taken the opportunity to hone in on what it will take to accomplish your goals, now is the time to do so.

Sacrifices will be a part of your journey. Just like you can't walk into your favorite department store and shop without paying, you can't walk through life expecting to receive all the finer things for free. There is a cost for whatever it is that you want and every goal that you want to achieve. If you want good grades, you can't party every night. If you want your start-up to succeed, rest assured you'll have many sleepless nights. If you want to maintain a superb reputation, you can't do everything everyone else does, no matter how exciting it may seem at the time.

Also understand that the cost for some goals is greater than for others. For example, earning an A in a class takes a lot more effort than earning a C. Getting six-pack abs requires much more discipline than it does to just "stay fit." Making an Olympic team is a lot harder than making a high school team. Placing 50% of your paycheck into a savings account takes a greater amount of self-control than just placing 10%. And buying a brand new Maserati will require better financials than purchasing a five-year-old Honda Accord. It is crucial that once you have set goals for yourself, that you are not only realistic about the costs, but you are also willing to pay them. At the end of the day, you can't have a million dollar dream with a minimum wage work ethic.

> *"If you want something you've never had before, you've got to do something you've never done before."* –Coco Chanel

No matter what the cost for your goals may be, an important thing for you to do is to remember the purpose in what you are doing. Remember your goals, and think of the joy that you will have when you achieve them. Yes, studying may be hard. You may sacrifice a social life and spend most of your time with your nose in a book. But how amazing will it feel when you are holding that degree in your hand? Yes, being a mom is the hardest job in the world. But don't you feel awesome each time your child reaches a milestone? Yes, starting your own business is often stressful. You lose sleep. You may even lose some "friends." But imagine the liberation you will feel when the business is successful and you are financially free. That's why it's so significant to keep a vision of the positive results that will come from your sacrifices (i.e., vision board). When you understand the purpose in what you are doing, and you can envision the positivity that will result from you pursuing your goals, you will see that it becomes that much easier to keep moving forward.

There are no shortcuts to achieving your goals. It will take development and preparation in order to reach your desired end. It is easy to get impatient when you've created a vision for your life and nothing seems to be manifesting. Many times, when we've set a goal, we want it to come to pass as soon as possible; however, most achievements require a process. In the fifth grade, when you decided you wanted to graduate from high school, you couldn't walk across that stage the next day. You had to finish elementary school and middle school first. Then you had to pass all of your high school classes, as well as pass the exit exam. Only after you successfully made it through every stage were you able to accomplish your goal of graduation.

The same is true in life. You will have to pass certain tests in order to achieve success. You will have to experience certain things that will allow you to appreciate and take full advantage of the goal you are trying to reach.

Consider Oprah. She's one of the most successful women in the entire world, but her life hasn't always been enviable. Before becoming a multi-billionaire, Oprah endured a rough childhood during which she not only experienced severe poverty, but also suffered physical and sexual abuse. At nine years old, she was raped for the first time, and the abuse continued for years. At fourteen, she became pregnant with a child who died shortly after childbirth. In high school, things began to turn around for Oprah. She began to thrive academically and discovered her love for media. She earned a full scholarship to Tennessee State University, but left early to pursue her media career.

At age twenty-two, Oprah arrived in Baltimore, Maryland to take a prestigious job as a co-anchor on one of the local stations. Almost immediately, however, she noticed the hostility and was often treated with disrespect. She didn't have the job eight months before she was publicly fired. After getting removed from the anchor desk, Oprah performed a series of other jobs, including news writing and street reporting. Throughout this time, she was taken advantage of and sexually harassed. She also realized that she simply wasn't good at writing television news.

While Baltimore created many negative memories for Oprah, everything wasn't all bad. She not only met Gayle King, who remains her best friend to this day, but she was also able to eventually co-host the morning talk show "People are Talking." After a while, she ended up moving to Chicago and landed the gig hosting "AM Chicago." Within months, Oprah turned the show from being the lowest-rated talk show in Chicago to the highest-rated one. Three years later, it was named "The Oprah Winfrey Show."

Looking at Oprah's story raises many questions. If she hadn't struggled as a child, would she have been as driven to achieve such an enormous level of success? If she never moved to Baltimore, would she have ever met Gayle, who has proven to be her best and most loyal friend? If she hadn't been sexually abused, would she have grown to become such a powerful advocate for sexual abuse survivors? If she hadn't been mistreated as an employee, would she have become such a progressive boss? If she hadn't seen so many lows, would she have fully appreciated her amazing highs?

Sometimes, things can get frustrating, and the tests of life can be hard; however, you must persevere. Have faith that all of your experiences are preparing you to achieve the goal you have already claimed for yourself.

"There are no shortcuts to any place worth going." –Beverly Sills

Think about the Chinese bamboo tree. In the first season that it is planted, it doesn't grow but an inch. In its second season, it is watered and fertilized, but it still hardly grows. In its third season, the same thing happens. By its fourth season, it still hasn't grown. But in its fifth season, something amazing happens. It grows up to 80 feet! So why does nothing happen for four whole years? The truth of the matter is that something does happen. All along, the tree is getting ready for the massive growth that it will experience in its fifth year. The roots are growing, gaining strength, and becoming prepared to support the potential magnitude of the tree.

Remember the story of the Chinese bamboo as you go through your process of being prepared to reach your goals. Even when it seems like nothing is happening, know that you are being equipped with the necessary tools to reach your full potential. You just have to make sure you keep doing the right things and stay on the path to success. (Remember, the farmer still has to water and fertilize the bamboo tree even though it shows no sign of growth.)

As you continue to develop as a person on your journey to achieving your goals, don't become discouraged. As people, we've grown accustomed to getting things "now." We have fast food, microwaves, lotteries, ten-minute miracles, and one-day diets. With all of these things, sometimes we forget that success involves a process. But there is something we must remember: There will be no shortcuts.

Prosperous Points

- Set short-term goals that relate to your long-term goals. This will help to keep you on track to achieving your desired end.

- Don't set your short-term goals too high. You don't want to become discouraged. You simply want to have a way to measure the progress toward your bigger goals. Remember, you can always create new short-term goals when you achieve them.

- Don't set your long-term goals too low. You should always be sure you are challenging yourself. Challenges force you to grow and help you to reach your full potential.

- Write down your goals. You don't want to limit your goals to being just thoughts. Make them tangible.

- Tell your goals to someone you trust. This should be someone who can encourage you when times get hard and hold you accountable for what you want to do with your life.

- Claim your goal. You have to believe in yourself, or no one else will.

- Visualize. Imagine yourself accomplishing your goals. There is power in the mind!

- Create a vision board. Keep a physical representation of your goals in a place that you see every day. Use pictures, quotes, drawings, and whatever else you would like.

- Don't get caught up in the "how." Remember that you don't have to see the full staircase to take the first step. The most important thing is that you begin with a clear focus;

you do not have to know exactly how you are going to reach your desired end.

- Open your eyes. Be aware of what it will really take to achieve success. You can't expect to achieve your goals if you remain enclosed in your own bubble.
- Realize that you will make sacrifices on your journey. Everything has a cost. The important thing is to remember the benefits of the costs.
- Remember, there are no shortcuts to achieving your goals. All of your achievements will involve a process.

BRING THE HOUSE DOWN
(Give your all. All the time.)

I once heard the story about a young girl who was fascinated with achieving success. She wanted success so desperately that one day she approached the town's wisest philosopher to ask her about the true secret to becoming successful.

"Are you sure you want success?" the wise woman asked.

"Yes, I want it," the girl replied.

"How sure are you?"

"I'm very sure."

"Then come with me into the river."

The girl was confused, but she followed the wise woman into the nearby river. When the level of the water reached their necks, the philosopher took the girl by surprise, quickly pushing her head down under the water. The girl immediately began to struggle as she tried to keep from drowning, but the woman kept her submerged. The fight continued, and just as the girl was about to pass out, the philosopher pulled her above the water. Gulping deep breaths of air, the girl asked hoarsely why the wise woman had tried to kill her. She replied with a question.

"What is it that you most wanted when you were underwater?"

"I wanted to breathe," said the young girl, still gasping for breath.

"That's the secret of success. When you want success as bad as you wanted to breathe, then you will achieve it."

We all want success, whether it's in school, a career, or a relationship. But sometimes it can be easy for us to forget how hard we must work to achieve it. Success isn't going to come easily. At least not the type of success I know you want as a passionate woman. You're going to have to work hard and give your all in everything that you do. There's no other way around it.

Famed poet Robert Frost once said, "There are two kinds of people: some willing to work, and the rest willing to let them." I want you to be a part of the first group of people. No matter what, work hard. Don't worry; it will pay off. And you will ultimately be recognized for your efforts.

Understand that visualization is not the end of the story. Visualization is a huge part of success. In fact, you can't accomplish anything unless you first create the image of achievement in your mind. However, there's more to the recipe of achieving prosperity than visualization. Just like there's more ingredients needed to bake a cake besides flour. Yes, you have to visualize the end result. Yes, you need to constantly be setting and achieving goals. Yes, you need to claim your goals. And yes, you should take the time to create a vision board. But it doesn't stop there. Because at the end of the day, you can't just go around wishing that the pieces of your life would fall together. You have to actually do something.

*"I didn't get there by wishing for it, or hoping for
it, but by working for it."* –Estèe Lauder

Don't procrastinate. Easier said than done, right? I know, I know. But if you really want to achieve prosperity, you have to avoid letting procrastination take over your life. Because guess what? We are all given twenty-four hours in each day! You, me, Oprah Winfrey, J.K. Rowling, Melinda Gates, Sheryl Sandberg, Michelle Obama, Beyoncé, and everyone else! We are all given twenty-four hours! The question then becomes, "What are you doing with yours?"

Are you doing everything that you possibly can to make your dreams come true? Or are you waiting around for things to happen in your life? Are you taking the best action to achieve your goals? Or are you putting off until tomorrow what you could have actually done today?

You have dreams. You have goals. You have desires. You want to be great. We've established that. But you have to be willing to put forth the effort each day in order to get to where you want to be. If you want to finish writing your first book, start writing! If you want to start your own business, start putting together a business plan! If you want enough money in your savings account to buy a new house, start saving! If you need to ace your next exam, start studying! If you want to tone your body, start working out!

There is always an action that you can take to help you get to the next level. You just have to be willing to follow through. Even when it's hard. Even when it's scary. You have to follow through. This doesn't mean that you have to go out into the world and try to do everything. It simply means that you need to do *something*.

For example, if you want to write a book, don't put it off because you feel the task is too big. Start by writing a paragraph. That paragraph will eventually turn into five paragraphs, which will eventually turn into a whole chapter, which will eventually turn into three chapters... You get the point. But the lesson here is that you can't accomplish anything by always putting tasks off until tomorrow. You have to start today, even if the task is something small.

Each and every day, I challenge you to do something that your future self will thank you for. No matter how big or small, DO SOMETHING. Take action! Get the ball rolling! There is something that you can do right now that will bring you closer to achieving your goals. So, do it! Why wait? You're not getting any younger, and life has no problem passing you by.

Procrastination not only hinders the achievement of your goals, but it also often leads to unnecessary stress. What if you wait until the last minute to print that huge report, and your printer stops working? What if you only have one more submission to make, and the Internet goes down? What if there's an accident on your commute to that huge job interview? What if you wait until the day before your mom's birthday to get her the gift she's been asking for all year, and then you find that it's sold out? What if you meet someone who could help take your career to the next level, but due to your procrastination, you don't have anything to present to him or her? Awful, right? Keep these things in mind when you want to put off tasks that you could start today!

Stop making excuses. If you wanted to, you could come up with a million excuses right now as to why you can't achieve prosperity and reach your goals. You're too tall. You're too short. You don't have enough money. No one believes in you. You don't know the right people. You aren't smart enough. You're too young. You're too old. The task requires too much work. There's not enough time. You don't have the education. You don't feel motivated. You don't know where to start. The list could go on, and on, and on…

So how exactly is an excuse different from an actual reason? Well, a true "reason" is just that. It is a genuine explanation for why something is the way it is. For example, if Amanda left extra early for work but, unfortunately, got into a minor car accident (in which she was not at fault), then THAT'S the reason why she'd be late or absent from her job that day. But if she always waits until the last minute to leave to go to work, "morning traffic" would not be a reason. It's an excuse. If she knew she had to be on time, then she should have left earlier to account for the normal morning traffic! The traffic isn't what made her late. Her refusal to leave at an appropriate time made her late.

The same is true for things that are seemingly out of our control. We have control over more things than we give ourselves credit for. No, you can't change who your parents are. You can't help how much money you had growing up. You can't help the situation you were born into. You can't change your biology. In fact, there are many things we can't change. And it's okay! Just because we can't change something doesn't mean it has to hinder us. Because, guess what? No one can go back and start a new beginning, but anyone can start today and make a new ending. You can control the decisions you choose to make every day that are either going to take you closer or farther away from your dreams.

When you have a goal that you want to accomplish, the excuses have to go! Stop thinking of all the reasons why something can't be done, and start thinking about all of the reasons why it can! It's time to take responsibility for your future and refuse to let anything else get in the way.

"The difference between successful people and others is how long they spend time feeling sorry for themselves." —Barbara Corcoran

Pay attention. There once was a merchant who sent his son to learn the Secret of Happiness from the wisest of men. The young man wandered through the desert for forty days until he reached a beautiful castle at the top of a mountain. There lived the sage for whom the young man was looking.

However, instead of immediately finding the sage, the young man entered a room and saw a great deal of activity; merchants coming and going, people chatting in the corners, a small orchestra playing sweet melodies, and there was a table laden with the most delectable dishes of that part of the world.

The wise man talked to everybody, and the young man had to wait for two hours until it was time for his meeting. The sage listened attentively to the reason for the boy's visit, but told him that at that moment he did not have the time to thoroughly explain to him the Secret of Happiness.

He suggested that the young man take a stroll around his palace and come back in two hours' time.

"However, I want to ask you a favor," the wise man added, handing the boy a teaspoon in which he poured two drops of oil. "While you walk, carry this spoon and don't let the oil spill."

The young man began to climb up and down the multiple palace staircases, always keeping his eyes fixed on the spoon. By the end of the two hours, he had traveled all around the estate, so he returned to the presence of the wise man.

"So," asked the sage, "did you see the Persian tapestries hanging in my dining room? Did you see the garden that the Master of Gardeners took ten years to create? Did you notice the beautiful parchments in my library?"

Embarrassed, the young man confessed that he had seen nothing. His only concern was not to spill the drops of oil that the wise man had entrusted to him.

"So, go back and see the wonders of my world," said the wise man. "You can't trust a man if you don't know his house."

Now more at ease, the young man took the spoon and strolled again through the palace, this time paying attention to all the works of art that hung from the ceiling and walls. He saw the gardens, the mountains all around the palace, the delicacy of the flowers, the taste with which each work of art was placed in its niche, and all of the beauty throughout the estate grounds. Returning to the sage, he reported in detail all that he had seen.

"But where are the two drops of oil that I entrusted to you?" asked the sage.

Looking down at the spoon, the young man realized that he had spilled the oil.

"Well, that is the only advice I have to give you," said the sage of sages. "The Secret of Happiness lies in looking at all the wonders of the world and never forgetting the two drops of oil in the spoon."

Wow! Powerful, right? I first read this story by Paulo Coelho (author of *The Alchemist*) years ago, and it has always stuck with me. In describing "the secret of happiness," this story explains the significance of being able to pay attention to the task at hand without losing sight of life's other treasures.

Paying attention isn't often easy. There are always distractions that can deter us from our goals. But putting forth the effort to be present in all areas of your life will allow you the distinct opportunity to attain prosperity. When you are faced with a tough work project, do you still notice when your child is struggling in school? When your relationship is going through a rough patch, are you still paying attention to your business? When you are bogged down with life, do you still look for the beauty in your adversity?

Yes, it takes effort to truly pay attention to all the varying aspects of your life at one time. It's easy to focus in on one facet (like the two drops of oil) and fail to see everything else that is going on around you (like the beauty of the mansion). But as women, we inherently wear multiple hats. And having the ability to truly be present in all of the important areas of our lives will determine the level of prosperity we will be able to achieve in those areas.

The irony of being expected to pay attention to multiple things at one time is that it is actually almost impossible for humans to completely focus on more than one thing at any given moment. Yes, you read that correctly. A huge determining factor in finding prosperity in all aspects of your life is dependent on your ability to be present in each of those aspects; however, you can't literally focus on everything at one time. So, what should you do? One word: Categorize.

When you wear multiple hats, it is absolutely imperative to categorize the major areas of your life. If you don't, it is easy to forget where to place your attention. For example, at any given time, I am able to list off the main categories of my life where I choose to place a majority of my attention. Whenever I get bogged down and feel unsure of what I need to do, I say that list in my head. Right now, that list is: faith, family, books, speeches, movie, business, fun. Whether it's 1:00 am or 1:00 pm, I can always recollect that list, and I make sure that I do something significant each day in each of those categories. That is how I "pay attention" to the various facets of my life.

When I say the word "faith," I think of something that I need to do for the day that will bring me closer to God. Sometimes I go in a quiet room and pray. Sometimes I open my Bible app to read before a meeting. Other times I'll take the time to watch a sermon. When I say "family" to myself, I often think of the people close to me that I need to reach out to or for whom I need to do something special. And I don't just think about it. I actually pick up my phone to make a phone call or send a text message. I use that time to set up lunch dates and let my family know how much I care. The same is true with "books, speeches, movie, and business." I pick at least one thing to do that will bring me closer to accomplishing a short-term or long-term goal in those categories. Then when I get to the word "fun," I choose something that will bring me joy. Whether I dedicate a few hours to a category or a few minutes, I make sure I do something each day! In this way, I'm always sure that days do not pass in which I am not present in all of these areas of my life.

We've already established that you wear many different hats. Whether you're a wife, mother, student, entrepreneur, or all of the above, there are many facets of your life in which you are expected to be present. And I'm not going to lie to you and say that it's easy to do. But an important aspect of your ability to achieve prosperity in more than one part of your life will be your capacity to devote attention to more than one thing at one time. Create categories, and be purposely present in each of those categories. See the castle, but still pay attention to those two drops of oil!

Don't take shortcuts. In any situation, there is often both an easy way to go about completing a task and a hard way. In most cases, it just makes sense to take the easy way. For example, why drive through traffic if there is a less busy road you can take? Sure, you could argue that sitting in traffic and dealing with reckless drivers may help to build your character, but is it really necessary? I'm going to go out on a limb here and say that it's not.

The same is true for many of life's mundane tasks. I'll bet the last time you wanted to research a topic you didn't go to the library to use an encyclopedia. You probably whipped out your phone and did a quick online search. And why not? The Internet is faster and available right at your fingertips. Why make your life harder when it doesn't need to be?

When I say to never take shortcuts I don't mean to always find the hardest way to go about doing things. Honestly, that would be idiotic. What I mean is that you have to be committed to your growth process. True success not only takes time and effort, but it takes the discipline to understand that certain steps have to be taken to achieve various goals. If you want to be a doctor, it's probably not a good idea to cheat your way through school. You need to know every required concept if you're going to get into medical school, pass your boards, and become a well-respected medical professional. The same is true in life regardless of your passion or occupation. In anything you choose to pursue, don't cheat yourself. Use every experience as an opportunity to learn more and become more.

Success doesn't come easy. We have to work for it. And sometimes we can want it so bad that we skip over steps A, B, and C just to get to D faster. We do this without realizing that the keys to unlock doors in step D were sprinkled throughout the previous steps. If you want to sustain your prosperity, you have to obtain the tools in order to do so. Do chefs bring your meal out before they are finished cooking it? No! Even if you're starving and you're ready to eat, you have to wait until the chef is done with her work. If you *insist* that the chef bring out the unfinished food because you just can't wait, you'll probably end up complaining and sending it back anyway. So you might as well wait on the food to finish. Are you catching my drift here?

There are things that I was prepared for at twenty-one years of age that I would not have been ready for at sixteen. There are things I'm able to tackle now that I wouldn't have been able to at twenty-one. And I'm sure there are things that I will be more equipped to handle ten years from now (God-willing) than I am today. The same goes for you. Yes, sometimes things take time. And no, it's not always easy to wait. But the best thing you can do in order to truly enjoy the end results is commit to the process of your growth.

"There's no such thing as an overnight success." —Tory Burch

Do what others won't do. If you want exceptional results, you have to give exceptional effort. You can't go through life doing everything that everyone else does and expect different outcomes. It just doesn't work that way.

One of my favorite quotes is by NFL Hall of Famer, Jerry Rice. He once said, "Today, I will do what others won't so that tomorrow I can accomplish what others can't." Ponder that for a moment. One of the most celebrated athletes in sports owes his success to waking up each day and doing things that others simply won't do.

If everyone in your study group is only doing enough to pass the class, put in the extra effort to earn an A. If your coach says to do ten reps of an exercise, do fifteen. If your colleagues wake up at 7:00 am, wake up at 6:00 am. At least once a week, I challenge you to ask yourself, "Am I really doing everything I possibly can to achieve my goals?" If the answer is "no," get to work! I've said it before, and I'll say it again. True prosperity does not come easy. You have to really work for it.

Let's face it. The world is competitive! You're not the only one who wants to be valedictorian, receive the job promotion, earn the prestigious grant, get the degree, start a successful business, raise positive and fruitful kids. There are other women who want the same things that you do. And when you aren't working as hard in certain areas of your life as you need to, there is always someone else who is willing to step up. If you want extraordinary results, you have to be willing to give extraordinary effort. Go above and beyond. Your future self will certainly thank you for it.

Leave your fear behind. Many times, we make excuses because we're afraid. Whether it's a fear of failure, fear of change, or fear of success, often it is fear that essentially keeps us from reaching our destiny.

If failure is your biggest fear, you have to let it go! Failure is an unavoidable part of life. Everything will not always go your way, and sometimes things just don't work out. But failure is only temporary. And it's no reason to refrain from going after your goals. Without failure, there would be no success. Disappointment often teaches us valuable lessons, and it also allows us to truly appreciate success when it comes. Don't shy away from failure. Embrace it. And definitely don't fear it.

In addition to failure, change is also a common fear that keeps us from achieving success. And just like failure, change is a natural part of life. Yes, sometimes it's unexpected. Sometimes it hurts. Sometimes, we just don't want to go through the process. But change allows us to grow. It gives us the opportunity to gain new experiences and develop outside of our comfort zones. Don't let the fear of change keep you from doing everything you need to do to make your dreams come true!

While it's easy to comprehend why a person may fear failure or change, it is often harder to understand why a person may actually fear success. After all, who doesn't want to be successful? Yes, everyone has an inherent desire to be great, but many of us are actually scared of success without even realizing it. Perhaps it's because some of us don't want to be in the spotlight. Or maybe it's because we're scared of what other people might think. We might even think we don't deserve success. But that is not true! You deserve success! And you deserve to know that you are worth it.

Marianne Williamson said it best: "Our deepest fear is not that we are inadequate. Our deepest fear is that we are powerful beyond measure. It is our light, not our darkness that most frightens us. We ask ourselves, 'Who am I to be brilliant, gorgeous, talented, and fabulous?' Actually, who are you not to be? You are a child of God. Your playing small doesn't serve the world. There is nothing enlightened about shrinking so that other people won't feel insecure around you. We are all meant to shine, as children do. We were born to make manifest the glory of God that is within us. It's not just in some of us; it's in everyone. And as we let our own light shine, we unconsciously give other people permission to do the same. As we are liberated from our own fear, our presence automatically liberates others."

Find additional resources. As I always say, "If you really want to do something, you'll find a way. If you don't, you'll find an excuse." This specifically applies to your dreams and goals. Stop saying that you don't have the resources. Or you don't know the right people. Or you don't have enough education. Or you don't have a mentor. Go after what you want and make it happen!

I remember when I was taking a difficult course in college. The professor was extremely smart, but seemed to have trouble teaching the concepts in a way that the students could understand. Each class period, students would complain about how they couldn't comprehend the concepts and how they were definitely going to fail the class. I could've joined in on the complaints, but I decided to take matters into my own hands.

After each class, I would go online and research the academic concepts. I'd find notes, videos, and discussions that would help shed light on the theories. I took quizzes online, and I took my own notes from the information I found on other university websites. It took a lot of effort, but the results paid off. By using outside resources, I ended with the highest grade in the class, and I was exempt from taking the final exam!

My final grade in that economics class was earned purely through hard work and resourcefulness. I didn't end with the highest grade because I was smarter than anyone else. I am sure there were plenty of people in that class smarter than I. But I was willing to go above and beyond, which made all the difference in the world. The same is true in life. Sometimes you have to think outside of the box. It often isn't good enough to only use the resources that are right in front of you. In fact, it can be frustrating when it seems as if the tools you have to work with just aren't enough. Don't give up on your dreams when this happens. Keep pushing forward, and keep working hard. Just open yourself up to other avenues to help you achieve your goals.

Guess how I learned the process of writing screenplays? Google. I never went to school for film or screenplay writing, but I always had a dream of writing movies. For weeks, I spent every waking moment researching screenplay elements and reading popular scripts. I then bought scriptwriting software and started composing my very first screenplay. Years later, when I was just nineteen years old, I sold that very same screenplay. Like I said, if you really want to do something, find a way!

Ask questions. If you don't know something, ask. Sounds simple enough, but too often we go without getting the help we need just because we are afraid to ask. I remember when I was in middle and high school, I used to HATE asking questions. Everyone knew me as the "smart girl," so I always felt "less than" when I needed to raise my hand. Instead of just asking questions when I did not know the answer, I would go home and teach myself what I needed to know.

At such a young age I had developed a horrible habit of not asking questions when they needed to be asked. It would be years before I would truly realize that asking questions isn't a sign of weakness. Instead, it is a tool by which we become more aware of the world around us and gain deeper understanding of people and issues.

There's no point in working hard toward something if you don't understand what you're doing or why you're doing it. Ask questions if you are unsure. Prosperous women ask questions, because they know that it is actually a sign of strength and intelligence, not weakness. The most successful people in the world are aware of how much they don't know. Don't be afraid to ask questions to figure it out.

Have integrity. As you climb the ladder of success, you have to be sure that it is leaning against the right building. Don't worry if you see people who seem to get ahead in life by lying, cheating, and manipulating. It will catch up with them. Just continue to do the right thing, despite what others may do.

If you tell someone you are going to do something, do it. If you find yourself in a bad situation, get out before things become worse. Stay true to yourself and remain on the right path so that nothing can hinder you from reaching your full potential.

When you have integrity, you do the right thing even when no one is watching. Even when it is hard. Even when everyone else seems to be getting ahead using negative tactics. Women with high integrity always put forth the greatest amount of effort in everything that they do. They understand that the quality of their effort in all aspects of their lives says a lot about them as people.

No matter what situation may come your way, you have to stay strong and hang on to your values. Only success built on the right foundation will actually last.

"Real integrity is doing the right thing, knowing that nobody's going to know whether you did it or not." –Oprah Winfrey

Never confuse movement with progress. Some tasks keep us busy, but get us nowhere closer to where we want to be. For example, hanging out with your friends every night may keep you from getting bored, but is it helping you get closer to achieving your goals? Having repeated discussions with your colleagues about a work problem gives you the chance to further dissect the issue at hand, but is it bringing you closer to finding a solution? Praying about a situation is absolutely necessary, but are you putting the work behind your faith? Remember that you can run in place and still not go anywhere.

I meet people all the time who believe that being busy means they are being productive. It just doesn't work that way. Think about it. A chemistry teacher could give her students crossword puzzles to complete each day in class, which would keep them busy for an entire semester. But unless the students do something else, they will probably not pass the state exam at the end of the semester. This is true in life. Many times we get so caught up in "busy work" that we aren't actually doing the things that need to be done to accomplish our goals.

I remember hearing the story of an older lady who was having a hard time financially. She was very spiritual, so she went to the steps of her church every single day, often just to pray for groceries. She would lift her hands up to the sky and say aloud, "Lord, please help me through my hard times. All I need are some groceries to get me through!" After saying her prayer, she would go to work at her job down the street where she picked up extra hours. The next day, she was back at the church.

"Lord, help me! You know my struggles. Please have mercy on me!" As she said her prayers, an atheist who lived next door would chuckle. He often shouted back, "Why do you keep coming here every day to pray for groceries? There's no God! Your situation isn't going to change!"

Despite the man's negativity, the older lady kept returning to the church on her way to work. One morning, she was pleasantly surprised when she approached the church steps to see about ten bags of groceries sitting on the porch. She immediately shouted, "Lord, you have answered my prayers! Thank you, Lord! Thank you!!"

The atheist man shouted back, "I told you there was no

God! He didn't get you those groceries. I got you those groceries! You were getting on my nerves!"

The woman put her hands back up in the air to give more thanks: "Thank you, God! Not only did you get me groceries, but you made the devil pay for them!!!"

I tell this story often in my speeches. It never fails to make the audience laugh, and the message is very clear. At any given time, there is something that we really want. But no matter what our current situation, we have to remain diligent in our efforts to move forward. We have to continue doing the right things to bring us closer to our goals. We have to put the work behind our faith. It's easy to just "find something to do." But we have to make sure that our tasks have true purpose. This lady prayed on the steps of the church for groceries every day, but she never stopped going to work. She even picked up extra hours on her shift. Everything she did was meant to get her closer to where she needed to be. The atheist told her God wasn't listening, but she never gave up. Then, when she least expected it, the very person she thought was her "enemy" was used to get her exactly what she needed.

Stay focused, and remain diligent. Don't do things just because they will keep you busy. Perform tasks that will truly help you achieve your dreams. Prayer changes things, yes. But don't just pray without putting the work behind your prayer. Don't keep talking about a problem without putting forth the effort to find a solution. Don't only do crosswords when you should be learning actual chemistry.

Treat others the way you want to be treated. It's called the "golden rule" for a reason. Treating others the way you want to be treated isn't just the right thing to do in a diplomatic sense; it's the right thing to do if you are trying to live your best life. When you put out positive energy, you receive positive energy back. Therefore, when you treat people with love and respect, you invite people in your life to do the same for you. Have you ever been around people with a "magnetic" personality? They're nice, easy to get along with, and have a ton of friends. On the other end of the spectrum, have you ever been around individuals that "nobody likes"? They are rude, hard to get along with, and have very few friends. These two very different types of people perfectly demonstrate the dynamics of treating others the way you want to be treated. When you put out positivity (like the first group of people), you receive a positive response. When you put out negativity (like the second group of people), you receive a negative response. It's as simple as that.

Sometimes you may even have to be nice to people who are hard to be nice to. You know those types of people. They complain about everything. They always have something to say. They see the negative in every situation. They come across as being mean for no reason. It may be hard, but never give in to the temptation to treat them like they treat you. Resist the urge to talk them down to other people. Instead, love them. Be the best person you can be despite how they may act toward you.

You can't control the thoughts and actions of other people, but you can control your own. Regardless of how other people act, treat them like you would want to be treated. Don't stoop to the level of those who resort to constantly complaining, badmouthing, and being negative. Rise above, and be the best version of yourself that you can be.

"Great minds discuss ideas; average minds discuss events;
small minds discuss people." –Eleanor Roosevelt

Shut up and listen. God gave you two ears and just one mouth for a reason: Listen twice as much as you speak. As tempting as it may be to voice your opinion on every little thing, learn to listen to others who have the capability to help you on your journey to the top. Whether it's a professor, coach, family member, mentor, or friend, there are individuals who have your best interest in mind. They want to see you successful, and they have the wisdom to help make your dreams a reality. Listen to what they have to say, even if you don't always agree. And don't just pretend to listen. Appreciate words of guidance and different perspectives.

Someone once told me, "If you want to be liked by people, listen. If you want to learn something, listen. If you want success, listen." So guess what? I listen. Yes, sometimes it's extremely hard not to cut people off and jump to conclusions. But I've learned that interrupting is often just a waste of time. The speaker gets frustrated, and you are ultimately prevented from obtaining a full understanding of what they're trying to say. This means that even when the tensions are high, you have to make the conscious effort to listen to the other person. If both of you are simply refusing to hear the other's point of view, nothing will get resolved, and you will be a prisoner to your own perspective.

I remember a time when one of my employees got really upset with me about something she *thought* I did. When she decided to inform me of why she was so dismayed, I was completely appalled. She had created an entire scenario in her head based on bits and pieces of incorrect information she patched together. Being her boss, I could have easily rejected her explanation. After all, her approach was extremely negative and, in my head, unwarranted. But I didn't cut her off. I let her finish. I let her explain. And when her entire perspective was laid out on the table for me to see, I digested the information and I responded. There are many things I could have said in my response, but I chose the higher road. I took each one of her points and offered an explanation; I could tell she felt better with each word I said. By the end of the conversation, she apologized for freaking out on me. I accepted the apology and moved on. After all, she had always been a dependable employee, and I know that as humans, we all have our moments.

Did I agree with my employee's approach? Absolutely not. Did I agree with her initial perspective? No. But I've always maintained an open mind, and I'm a strong believer that people deserve to be heard. I may not have understood why she was so upset (mainly because I hadn't actually done anything to her), but she was clearly offended. And knowing that I normally had a good working relationship with her, I felt it was my duty to seek understanding instead of quickly condemning her. Through our conversation, I realized that if I had communicated better with her in the beginning, she wouldn't have had the room to create all of those negative scenarios in her head. This realization didn't change her incorrect assumptions or her hostile approach; however, I decided to use the moment to pinpoint where I could further grow as a leader.

Sometimes it can be the hardest thing in the world to listen, especially when we don't agree with what is being said. But ultimately, there's beauty in seeking an additional perspective. There is always something to be learned, and there is always room for growth. Listening gives us that opportunity by opening our ears to thoughts and ideas outside of our own, allowing us to learn patience, solve problems, and truly value others.

"My dear brothers and sisters, take note of this:
Everyone should be quick to listen, slow to speak,
and slow to become angry." –James 1:19

Take responsibility. Make the realization that this is *your* life, not someone else's. So take responsibility for it. If you want something, go after it! Don't wait for someone else to tell you what you should be doing with your life. Decide today and hold yourself accountable. If you want success, take responsibility for the amount of effort you put into each day. Because it's not someone else's fault if you don't follow through with a plan to achieve your goals.

No one can live your life for you. You can try to blame other people and situations for why you aren't where you want to be, but it is ultimately your responsibility. You have to live every single day as if what you do matters, because it does! Every action you take helps to create the life you want (or don't want). So take ownership of what you choose to do each moment of each day.

Listen to yourself when you talk to others. Do you find yourself actively taking responsibility for outcomes? Do you tend to take more than your share of the blame when things go wrong? Or do you always point the finger toward someone or something else?

Regardless of the situation, prosperous women hold themselves accountable. If we want to unlock our full potential in all of the different aspects of our lives, we have to take full responsibility for our actions and be willing to put forth the effort to make our dreams come true.

"In the long run, we shape our lives, and we shape ourselves. The process never ends until we die. And the choices we make are ultimately our own responsibility." —Eleanor Roosevelt

Take advantage of opportunities. There once was a man who was drowning in the ocean. A boat came by to save him, but he said, "You don't have to save me. Jesus will." Another boat came by, and he said the same thing. "You don't have to save me. Jesus will." A third boat came by to save the drowning man, but he still had the same response. "You don't have to save me. Jesus will." Finally, a helicopter flew over the man's head, offering help. Still the man said, "You don't have to save me. Jesus will." Eventually, the man drowned and he went up to heaven. When he met with God, he was furious! He exclaimed, "How could You let me drown? You saw me there, drowning in the ocean!" God replied, "I sent you three boats and a helicopter. What more did you want me to do?!"

The sad part about this story is that many of us choose to live our lives in the same way. We wait, and we wait, and we wait, even when our opportunity is right there in front of us. Don't miss out on your destiny simply because you failed to recognize a great opportunity. Take advantage of every situation in an effort to get where you want to be. You only have one life. Don't miss out!

Do your best. Have you ever failed to do your best at something and felt bad about it later? Maybe you could've had a better work presentation, but you didn't practice going through all of your points. Maybe you could've gotten an A on that math exam, but you wanted to hang out with your friends the whole night before. Maybe you could've gotten your mom something better for her birthday, but you didn't make her special day a priority.

When you know you could have done better, it feels awful. Which is why it is important to always make the commitment to try your best. No matter what it is that you are trying to achieve in life, it is important that you always give your all.

When I was younger, my mom gave me one of the best pieces of advice I have ever received. I was getting ready for a gymnastics competition when I asked her, "What if I don't get first place?" She looked at me, fully understanding my question. She knew that I worked hard each and every day to be on top, so what would it mean if I didn't win? Was I not working hard enough? Was I not good enough? Without missing a beat, my mom gave me a confident reply. She said, "Rae-Rae, you can't always worry about coming in first place. On any given day, someone's best may be better than your best. But if you give it your all, then that's all you can do."

My mom was right. Trying your best doesn't always mean that you'll get first place. It doesn't always mean that you'll get the job. It doesn't always mean you'll accomplish your goal the first time. It doesn't always mean that people will appreciate your efforts. What it does mean, however, is that you can be proud of yourself. You can keep moving forward, knowing that there was nothing else you could have done. You will have no regrets, and if you continue on this positive path, you will end up exactly where you need to be. One of my favorite songs has a line that says, "After you've done all you can, you just stand." In other words, when you have given your all, just stand up with satisfaction and keep confidently marching toward your goals.

Let go of the past. You can never start the next chapter of your life if you keep rereading the last one. In order to truly move forward with your dreams and goals, you have to be willing to let go of any past mistakes, hurts, and transgressions. Each day, we have the ability to start fresh and shrug off the issues of the past. But the problem is that many of us choose to hold onto previous situations that we can no longer control.

Letting go can be extremely difficult. Whether it's a person, habit, idea, expectation, or experience, we tend to find comfort in what's familiar, even if it is doing us no good. We may fantasize what could've been with our last romantic partner, even though deep down we know the relationship was toxic. We may continue with a bad habit, because it makes us feel good in the moment. We may hold on to certain expectations, because we can't imagine going down a different life path. We may even refuse to let go of a tragic experience, because we find security in being the victim.

What I have found in my talks with numerous women around the world is that many of us would rather be certain we're miserable than risk being happy. We often find ourselves in situations where we are holding on to things that are undoubtedly keeping us from a state of prosperity. Break this cycle today! Understand that the only way to accept new happiness in your life is to make space for it. Whatever it is that you are holding onto, let it go!

Can you imagine driving down the road while only looking through your back window? It simply can't be done. You may be able to move forward a few feet without getting into an accident, but sooner or later you have to look forward if you want to avoid a crash. The same is true in life. It's basically impossible to move forward if your focus is on what's behind you. Live your life by looking through the windshield, not the rearview mirror. Keep your eye on the prize and let go of anything in the past that's trying to keep you from achieving your dreams!

"Instead of looking at the past, I put myself ahead 20 years and try to look at what I need to do now in order to get there then." —Diana Ross

Give back. The people who realize that life is not all about them see greater levels of success than others can even imagine. Take Oprah for example. She's one of the most successful women in the world, but she doesn't keep her billions to herself. Yes, she lives a comfortable life, but she makes it a point to give others opportunities to become the best they can be. She has donated hundreds of millions of dollars to educational causes and has started multiple initiatives to give people the tools they need to succeed in the classroom and in life. And who can forget the time she gave every member of her audience a brand new car? Oprah doesn't only use her platform to give back, but she also encourages others to do the same. On one episode of her talk show, she gave more than 300 members of her audience $1,000 each to give to their favorite charity. What I love most about Oprah is that her philanthropic efforts don't stop with monetary donations. She has established her own charitable foundations and personally created programs to serve underprivileged individuals.

As a prosperous woman, you already know that the world does not revolve around you. There are other individuals out there who could use your help and who would appreciate your attention. There are plenty of ways to give back. You could donate to an organization, volunteer your time, cook for someone in need, give blood, mentor a student, help build a house, or run for a cause. The list goes on and on. Each day is filled with opportunities to help make this world a better place. Whether you give someone a free lunch, a hug, or a smile, always make a conscious effort to contribute to others. It will make you feel good. I promise.

Realize that God's plans are not always your plans. This is a hard one. I've spent this entire chapter telling you how important it is to give your all in every aspect of your life if you want to achieve prosperity. But here's the kicker. No matter how bad you want to achieve something, the only way it will work out is if it is in alignment with God's plan for your life.

Does this mean to stop working? No! In order to achieve anything in life, you have to be willing to put in the corresponding effort. But often our plans simply pale in comparison to what God has in store for us. We may think that a particular success is a destination, while He sees it as a launching pad for further greatness. It doesn't mean that all of your hard work is irrelevant. It just means that sometimes your work will be used to accomplish something greater.

Maybe you wanted a relationship to work out more than anything in the world. You put in an enormous amount of effort. You loved your significant other just like you were supposed to. But it still didn't work out. If you truly did all that you could do, then you have to trust that God has something better in store for you. The lessons you learned from that relationship will stay with you for the rest of your life, so nothing is a waste. There is just better in store for you!

The same is true in all aspects of life. Just because you really want something and you work hard at it, doesn't mean it will always come to pass exactly how you envision it. But if you've been working hard and the plan happens to change, you better believe that something of significance will reveal itself soon.

I have a friend who learned at a very young age how this process works. In high school, he was one of the top football players in the country. He earned USA Today All-American Honors during his senior year and played in the U.S. Army All-American Bowl. Although he had his choice of colleges at which to play football, he chose the University of South Carolina. There, he made an immediate impact on the field, becoming one of the most recognized names in college football. Without a doubt, he was going to get drafted; his sites were set on playing in the NFL.

Unfortunately for my friend Marcus, he suffered a torn ACL during his sophomore year and a gruesome knee injury his junior year which consisted of a dislocated kneecap, torn ligaments, and nerve damage. He was drafted by the San Francisco

49ers; however, he was never able to recover as he hoped. He never played a game with the 49ers, and at the tender age of 23 was forced to retire from the sport he loved.

Marcus worked hard. He motivated his teammates. He listened to his coaches. He always strove to do the right thing. But God had something different in store. He started a charitable foundation and began speaking to youth all across the nation. Through his foundation, he created a program to help athletes stay on the right academic track in order to not only graduate, but get accepted into top universities. He has literally traveled the world, and he feels blessed that he now has the opportunity to impact more people than he could have ever imagined. He still uses football as a platform, but instead of playing in the NFL, he uses the sport to directly change kids' lives.

Yes, sometimes it hurts when things don't go as originally planned. But we have to trust the process. Consider Kerry Washington's story. An award-winning actress and producer, she is well-known for her role as Olivia Pope in the highly acclaimed television series *Scandal.* But did you know that before *Scandal,* she was actually cast in two other pilots? However, when networks picked up those two shows, Kerry was fired and recast. At the time, I am sure she was devastated. She had worked hard and prepared extensively for those roles. But both times, she was fired and overlooked for another actress. But God had bigger and better plans. She was soon hired as the leading actress in *Scandal,* and the rest is history. Yes, it's disappointing when things don't go our way. But we must trust that God's plans are better than our plans. As long as you're giving your best effort each and every day, you will end up exactly where you need to be.

Prosperous Points

- Understand that visualization is not the end of the story. At the end of the day, you can't just go around wishing that the pieces of your life would fall together. You have to actually do something.
- Don't procrastinate. We are all given twenty-four hours. What are you doing with yours?
- Stop making excuses. If you wanted to, you could come up with a million reasons right now as to why you can't achieve prosperity and reach your goals. Don't.
- Pay attention. Having the ability to truly be present in all of the important areas of our lives will determine the level of prosperity we will be able to achieve in those areas.
- Don't take shortcuts. The best thing you can do in order to truly enjoy the end results is commit to the process of your growth.
- Do what others won't do. If you want exceptional results, you have to give exceptional effort. You can't go through life doing everything that everyone else does and expect different outcomes.
- Leave your fear behind. Many times, we make excuses because we have fear. Let it go!
- Find additional resources. As I always say, "If you really want to do something, you'll find a way. If you don't, you'll find an excuse."
- Ask questions. If you don't know something, ask. Sounds simple enough, but too often we go without getting the help we need just because we are afraid to ask.

- Have integrity. Don't worry if you see people who seem to get ahead in life by lying, cheating, and manipulating. It will catch up with them. Just continue to do the right thing, despite what others may do.
- Never confuse movement with progress. Some tasks keep us busy, but get us nowhere closer to where we want to be.
- Treat others the way you want to be treated. When you treat others with respect, that's what you will get back.
- Shut up and listen. God gave you two ears and just one mouth for a reason: Listen twice as much as you speak.
- Take responsibility. This is YOUR life. Stop blaming other people and situations for your shortcomings.
- Take advantage of opportunities. You only have one life. Don't miss out!
- Always do your best. When you give your all, you will have no regrets.
- Let go of the past. You can never start the next chapter of your life if you keep rereading the last one.
- Give back. The people who realize that life is not all about themselves see greater levels of success than others can even imagine.
- Realize God's plans aren't always your plans. As long as you're giving your best effort each and every day, you will end up exactly where you need to be.

RECOGNIZE YOUR TRUE STRENGTH
(Realize that your mind is a powerful tool.)

A group of frogs was traveling through the woods when two of the frogs, Sarah and Haley, fell into a deep pit. When the other frogs crowded around the pit and saw how deep it was, they told the two fallen frogs that there was no hope for them. Despite being told that there was no hope, Sarah and Haley decided to ignore what the others were saying; they proceeded to try to jump out of the pit.

Although the two frogs were putting forth an enormous amount of effort, the group of frogs at the top of the pit were still saying that they should just give up. "You'll never make it out!" they shouted.

Eventually, Sarah took heed to what the others were saying, and she gave up, falling down to her death. The other frog continued to jump as hard as she could. Again, the crowd of frogs yelled at her to just give up and die. There was absolutely no way that she was going to make it out alive.

Haley just jumped even harder, finally making it out. When she got out, the other frogs were quite surprised. "We thought there was no way that you could make it out of there!"

As the group of frogs gathered around Haley, asking how she gathered enough strength to do the impossible, she explained to them that she was deaf. Because she couldn't hear, she had no idea that they were telling her to stop. She thought they were encouraging her the entire time!

Isn't it crazy how much of an impact our mindsets have on our success? If Haley knew the other frogs were actually yelling at her to stop (instead of cheering her on), she would probably have given up like Sarah and never made it out. Think about this in terms of the implications of the placebo effect. It occurs when doctors take two groups of people with the same health problem and administer medication to them. The thing is, only the first group actually receives the medication. The second group *thinks* they are receiving the medicine, but are in fact just taking a sugar pill. Amazingly, a majority of people in the second group report improvement in their health, even though they have not been given any actual medication. Basically, because they expect to feel better in their minds, their bodies start to really feel better. This proves not only how powerful the mind is, but the impact a strong mindset will have on you as you set out to achieve your goals.

Your mind is stronger than your body. It's a proven fact. Your mind is what tells your body what to do; therefore, you can't take any action without thinking about what you are going to do first. In other words, your mind literally drives your body. So what does this mean for you? It means that your body isn't what will keep you from achieving success. It's your mind. Ponder that for a second.

How many times have you given up in a workout when you start to feel a little pain? After you stop, most of the time you realize that if you really wanted to, you could have kept going. So what happened? Your mind gave up before your body did. You told yourself you were going to stop when you started to feel the burn, but your body was perfectly capable of continuing if you pushed it to do so.

"A woman is like a tea bag. You can't tell how strong she is until you put her in hot water." —Eleanor Roosevelt

I remember a time when I gave the gymnasts on my team an assignment called "Ten, Twenty, Ten." Basically, they use the gymnastics floor to sprint ten times, walk a lap, sprint twenty times, walk two laps, then sprint ten more times. The kicker is that everyone must complete each set of sprints in a specified amount of time. If they don't, they must repeat that set of sprints.

When the girls lined up to do their first set of ten sprints, I could tell they were already dreading the assignment. Sure enough, they missed time by two seconds, so I made them repeat the ten sprints after walking a lap. This time, they were two seconds early. Next, they had twenty sprints. Once again, they didn't pace themselves accordingly, and they didn't make time. One girl actually stopped around sprint sixteen and told me she couldn't do it. I told her she could, and I made her finish.

Since the girls didn't make time, they had to do the twenty sprints again. The tears started to roll. "We can't do this!" "If we didn't make it the first time, how are we supposed to make it now?!"

I replied, "Because it's mind over matter. You can do this. You're just telling yourselves that you can't. What are you going to do if you're at a competition, and you're tired on the last event? Are you just going to tell the judge you can't do it?"

"No," they said in unison.

"Okay, then. Let's go! And stop crying. It's harder to breathe when you're crying."

The girls started their twenty sprints. I looked at the stopwatch as they ran each line. They were definitely ahead of time.

"Good job, girls! You're almost there. I know it hurts. But push!" I encouraged.

Before they knew it, they were done. And they finished six seconds ahead of time. I used the moment for a quick motivational nugget.

"That's how I know these sprints are mental. If it was purely physical, there is no way you would've finished faster than you did the first time, after doing all of this running. No way."

The girls lined up to complete their last set of ten sprints. They finished even faster than they did the very first set of ten sprints.

"How did you finish that last set even faster than the first?" I asked.

"We don't know."

"Well, I know. When you started off, you had convinced yourself you were too tired to do it successfully, and guess what? That mindset caused you to fail. When you stopped feeling sorry for yourselves and had a more positive attitude, you finished faster, even after doing all of those extra sprints."

Later that night, I received a text message from one of my girls. "Thank you for pushing me and believing in me, even when I didn't believe in myself. You're a great coach."

That text message made my day, but I couldn't take all the credit. I explained to her that SHE was the reason she successfully finished the assignment. Yes, I may have encouraged her, but my words would not have mattered if she didn't convince herself that she could do it. Once she made up her mind that she was going to finish, that's exactly what she did. And that mindset is so true in all aspects of life.

How many times have you stopped pursuing a goal simply because you hit a few roadblocks along the way? How many times have you told yourself you couldn't accomplish a task just because it was going to be a bit of hard work? How many times have you allowed negativity to throw you off course?

If you want to be a prosperous woman, you have to have a strong mind. You have to understand that the journey to success is often filled with daunting tasks, but you cannot let that keep you from achieving your goals. You have to possess a mind that won't allow your body to give up, even when it seems impossible to keep moving forward.

Choose to have a good attitude. Famed motivational speaker Dennis S. Brown once said, "The only difference between a good day and a bad day is your attitude." I think these are some of the truest words ever spoken. When you break it down, life is all about perspective and how you choose to react to situations. If someone is rude to you, you don't *have* to be rude back. It's a choice. If someone does something nice for you, you don't *have* to return the favor. It's a choice. If you have a meeting at 8:00 am, you don't *have* to be on time. It's a choice.

Every day, you have a choice to be happy. No matter what

is going on around you, you can have a good attitude. But you cannot count on other people and circumstances to make you happy. Happiness comes from within. You can't say, "When I get married, *then* I'll be happy." "When my kid makes it through school, *then* I'll be happy." "When I get that promotion, *then* I'll be happy." "When my spouse acts right, *then* I'll be happy." Why? Because happiness does not come from success. Success comes from happiness. When you choose to be happy and you perform your activities with passion, you will realize your dreams. And instead of filling a hole, your success will add to the happiness you already have.

Never say that you can't make a positive choice. Understand that what you see depends primarily on what you look for. If you look for the good in people and situations, I can guarantee you'll find it. If you look for the bad in people and situations, I can guarantee you'll find that too. Stop giving your time to negativity and make an effort to find the positive in every situation. For example:

NEGATIVITY	POSITIVITY
I hate work.	I'm glad I have a job.
School is so hard.	I feel blessed I have the opportunity to further my education.
My mentor is always so hard on me.	I appreciate that I have a mentor who cares enough to help me become the best I can be.

That car accident up there is going to make me late!	I'm glad I wasn't a part of the accident. Let me find a detour.
I've never met my dad. Why would he do that to me?	My mom has always been my biggest fan.
Why did God let my aunt die of cancer?	I know that everything happens according to His plan, and I am happy my aunt no longer has to suffer.
I wish I was popular like her.	I may have a small circle of friends, but I know that I can truly count on them.
I've never done this before!	I have the opportunity to learn something new.
This is too complicated.	I'll look at this from a different perspective and get help if I need to.
There is no way this will work.	I will try my hardest to make this work.

You may be thinking, "It's not that easy. I can't be positive about EVERYTHING!" I beg to differ. No matter what the situation, you have a choice. You can choose to respond positively or react negatively. Keep in mind that I never said it would always be easy. Sometimes it may take everything you have to find the positive in a situation; however, you ALWAYS have a choice. It's up to you to choose the positive one.

Still not convinced? Take a look at the seemingly negative situations below that can be looked at in a positive way.

SITUATION	NEGATIVE REACTION	POSITIVE REACTION
Someone cuts you off.	"What the @$!%!"	"Somebody's in a rush. Good thing they didn't hit me. Let me continue with my great day."
Your significant other breaks up with you.	"My life is over! It wasn't even my fault!"	"It wasn't meant to be. I'll find someone who truly appreciates and loves me."
You didn't get the job.	"I'm just not good enough!"	"God is preparing me for something greater. I'll keep looking for opportunities."
Your best friend makes you mad.	"I'm never speaking to her again!"	"Everyone makes mistakes, and she has always been there for me. I'll forgive her."
Your grandma passes away.	"God, how could you take one of my favorite people away?!"	My grandma was an awesome person who taught me a lot. It was her time to go, but she will always live in my heart."

"If you don't like something, change it. If you can't change it, change your attitude." –Maya Angelou

Never make excuses. In the previous chapter, I wrote about the importance of not making excuses. In this chapter, I'll say it again. Stop making excuses! This is absolutely one of the worst things you can do. Why? Because as you make excuses, you are training your mind to believe that everything is always someone else's fault. And isn't it annoying to listen to people who have an excuse about everything?

"I would have been on time, but I was behind a slow car."

"I meant to call you back, but something came up."

"I would have gotten an A, but the professor doesn't know what he's talking about."

"It's not my fault I'm late. My alarm didn't go off."

"I'm not apologizing for that. You made me mad."

"I'll never get a promotion, because none of the supervisors like me."

In life, you have to learn to take full responsibility for your actions and not make excuses. If you make a mistake, own up to it. If you need to work harder, give that extra effort. If you want success, take control of your life and do what it takes to achieve it.

Never say something is impossible. If you want something bad enough, find a way to make it happen. It doesn't matter whether it's been done before or not. You can be the first. You cannot limit yourself with your own thoughts. Never doubt yourself. If you want something, go after it. Even if you're the first to do so. People will tell you no. People will tell you that it can't be done. People will tell you to set more realistic goals. The most important thing, however, is to believe in yourself. Believe that all your goals are attainable if you take the necessary steps to achieve them.

Women Who Did the Impossible

Dominique Moceanu: Who says you're too young to achieve your dreams? Moceanu never did. As a 14-year-old, she won an Olympic gold medal as a part of the 1996 U.S. Women's Gymnastics Team ("The Magnificent Seven"). Just a few months before, at age 13½, she became the youngest gymnast ever to win the all-around at the U.S. National Championships. Known for her difficult moves and energetic personality, Moceanu showed kids around the world that impossible was not in her vocabulary.

Venus and Serena Williams: These two tennis stars grew up in one of the most dangerous cities in the United States. But they didn't allow their surroundings to keep them from making something of their lives. The most famous sisters in tennis, they've won Olympic gold medals and have scored lucrative endorsement deals. Their success doesn't stop at tennis, however. As entrepreneurs, both sisters have been involved in various business ventures, including the acquisition of the Miami Dolphins as part owners. This move made them the first African-American women to acquire ownership of an NFL team.

J.K. Rowling: Famous for creating the *Harry Potter* book series, Rowling experienced an enormous amount of adversity while creating the wizarding world. She lost her mother to multiple sclerosis and struggled to support her daughter after getting divorced from her husband. When she was finally ready to send the first book off to be published, she was rejected by twelve different publishing companies! When a publisher eventually picked up the original *Harry Potter* book, the company suggested she change her name since the target audience of young males may not want to read a book written by a female. She decided to shorten Joanne Katherine to J.K., and the series took off! The book series turned into a film series, and a theme park of the fictional world was even created. Although it had never been done before, she became the world's first female billionaire novelist.

Helen Keller: Despite being both deaf and blind, she never allowed anyone or anything to hold her back. With the help of her teacher, Anne Sullivan, she was able to learn how to communicate with those around her. After eventually gaining acceptance into Radcliffe College (Harvard University), she went on to become the first deaf-blind person to earn a bachelor's degree at age 24. During her lifetime, she became a world-renowned author and motivational speaker, publishing twelve books and traveling the world giving inspirational talks.

> "You can waste your lives drawing lines. Or you can
> live your lives crossing them." –Shonda Rhimes

Don't believe the hype. People will always have something to say about the things you do, good or bad. But you have a choice of whether or not you're going to entertain the thoughts and opinions of others. It's funny. When you're down, people are often quick to criticize, and when you're up, those same people are often quick to praise. Be aware of this, and don't allow yourself to get caught up in the hype.

If someone says you aren't good enough, don't believe

them. I can assure you they're wrong. Did you know that Walt Disney was fired from one of his first animation jobs at a newspaper? Apparently, the editor told him that he lacked imagination and had no good ideas. Wow! Can you believe that? In his lifetime, Mr. Disney won twenty-two Academy Awards and pioneered many developments in the production of cartoons. Yet, when he was first starting out, he was told he wasn't good enough. What if he would've taken those negative words to heart? Can you imagine a world without *The Lion King, Toy Story, The Little Mermaid, Frozen*, and hundreds of other famous Disney titles? And who can forget about the cartoon that started it all: Mickey Mouse? Oh, and when is the last time you went to Disney World? Okay, you get my point.

It's okay if people doubt you. Use that doubt to help drive your success. Personally, I'm the type of person who loves to prove people's doubts wrong. As soon as someone tells me that my goals are unattainable, I work that much harder to show them otherwise.

Also understand that everyone will not approve of everything you do. And it's not your job to try to please everyone. It's your job to do the best you can with the tools you have been given. Let me tell you something. You could be the ripest, juiciest peach in the world, but there will still be people out there who don't like peaches. Never forget that.

Just as you can't believe those who doubt you or say you aren't good enough, you can't get caught up in the comments of those who think you're "the best thing since sliced bread." I once heard a person say, "Flatterers look like friends, just as wolves look like dogs." When someone gives you a compliment, you're appreciative, which is fine. However, you have to be aware that excessive praise can often do more harm than good, especially when that praise is insincere. Such flattery can throw you off if you start to believe that you are "just that good."

Don't get caught up in the hype. Appreciate the compliments of others, but beware of extreme flattery. Understand that there is always room for improvement, no matter where you are in your life or career. Just as you rise, you can easily fall. Thus be grateful for all of your successes and continue to work hard. Never take your achievements for granted.

Be different. Don't think that you have to be like everyone else. We all have different personalities and perspectives. We have all gone through different life experiences, which have worked together to shape us into the people we are today. No two people are exactly the same (even identical twins), so it doesn't make sense to go through your entire life trying to be like someone else.

It's good to be different. In fact, most people who make a difference in the world purposely shy away from the crowd. They realize that they have their own thoughts and beliefs, and they aren't intimidated by just being themselves.

One of the biggest challenges in life is trying to be your true self in a world that is trying to make you like everyone else. It can be hard to express your genuine identity when everyone around you has similar perspectives on life. But never forget that it is okay to be different! It is okay to have unique experiences and distinct opinions. Think about it this way: Perhaps God placed you (with all of your uniqueness) in a group of like-minded individuals for the purpose of offering a different point of view. Perhaps you are the person who can bring about positive change in your family or community, simply by expressing your true self! Don't shy away from the challenge.

Be a light in a world that has so much darkness. Be different in a time where many find comfort in being the same. At the end of the day, God made you an original. Don't die a copy.

> "In order to be irreplaceable, one must always be different." –Coco Chanel

Focus on what you want. Don't waste energy focusing on the things that you do not want. If you don't want to fail, don't focus on failing. Focus on succeeding. If you want to be financially free, don't focus on all of the money you currently don't have. Focus on the actions you must take to get to where you want to be. If you want a better relationship, don't focus on all of the things that your partner does that you don't like. Focus on having a good relationship.

Have you ever watched a game that started off close and ended in a blowout? The score was tied one minute. Then, soon after one team makes a mistake, the other team is winning by a landslide. Why does this happen? I can tell you why. The team that made the mistake is thrown off mentally. They lose momentum. They lose heart. They begin to think about the mistake as if it already cost them the game. They begin to focus not on how they are going to win, but how they are going to cover the deficit and keep from losing. Before long, they're headed back to the locker room disappointed and in tears.

Think about this in relation to your own life. Have you

ever had a day that started off bad and ended even worse? I know I have! It seemed like one bad thing happened, and then twenty more negative things followed. Then when a turn of events occurred and something good happened, twenty more good things happened. I am convinced this isn't by coincidence. Whatever you focus on in life (whether good or bad) will manifest. Believe that. So focus on the right things! Speak into existence the things that you want, and make the conscious effort to think positively in even the worst situations.

When focusing on the things that you want out of life, it is extremely important that you referee your thoughts. Every single manifestation begins with a thought. You have to learn to get rid of negative ideas, thoughts, and beliefs, and replace them with positive ones. By doing this, you will bring forth positive occurrences into your life, because your thoughts are immensely powerful. Trust me.

Watch your thoughts; they become words.
Watch your words; they become actions.
Watch your actions; they become habits.
Watch your habits; they become character.
Watch your character; it becomes your destiny.

-Frank Outlaw

Know your worth. If I offered you a crisp $100 bill right now, would you take it? Of course you would! Why wouldn't you take $100 with no strings attached? Exactly. Now, what if I crumpled up that same $100 bill and offered it to you? Would you still take it? Quite naturally, you would still accept the $100 bill. Why? Because even though it's crumpled up, you know that it is still worth $100.

The same is true with life. Sometimes our circumstances beat us up. Sometimes we feel crumpled by the pressures that surround us. Sometimes we forget our worth. But no matter what life throws your way, I promise that you will never lose your value.

It doesn't matter what you've gone through in life; God can still use you. The fact that you are still alive is proof that there is still more for you to do. Stop thinking that your past mistakes and negative experiences disqualify you from living a prosperous life. You are more than enough, and don't let anyone tell you otherwise.

Your mind is powerful. Never allow yourself to believe that your value is any less than the value of those around you. Your worth doesn't diminish due to people's inability to recognize it. Everything you have gone through has helped to make you the beautiful person you are today, as well as the prosperous woman you will continue to become. You are valuable. You are worthy. Don't ever forget it!

Be grateful. No matter what the situation, show appreciation. Be thankful that you're healthy. Be grateful for your talent. Give thanks for your supporters. Be appreciative of your upcoming success. Don't worry about what you do not have. Don't envy anyone else's gifts, talents, or possessions. Just give thanks for what you have been blessed with. As long as you appreciate the things that come to you, you will be provided with more things to appreciate. That's how life works.

You can improve the quality of your life right now by developing a mindset of gratitude. Practice appreciation daily, and watch how your life will change for the better. I guarantee that by giving thanks for all of the blessings in your life on a regular basis you will be more joyful and more peaceful.

As soon as you wake up in the morning, say thank you for being able to see another day. Before you eat a meal, say grace. When you accomplish a goal, give credit to those who helped you along the way. When someone does something nice for you, make sure they know you are grateful. Before you go to bed, give thanks for seeing the day all the way through. Whenever there is ever an opportunity, just say thanks! A simple "thank you" may seem like something so small, but it truly helps to renew your mind. I can't quite explain it, but it helps to cast a positive aura over your life even when it seems like so many things are going wrong. If you ever start to feel bad about how things are going in your life, try this: Make a list on a sheet of paper detailing all the things you are truly thankful for, whether it's a parent, a child, a job, your health, a new opportunity, or even just the breath in your body. After you're done making the list, read back over it. Then notice how you feel.

We are all given different things in life. No one has the same possessions or walks the same path. We all have different talents, abilities, experiences, and living situations. The key is to do what you can with what you have, appreciating every bit of it. Having gratitude doesn't mean that you are complacent. It doesn't mean that you should accept less than what you believe you deserve. It just means that while you are on your journey of accomplishing your goals, you're not looking down on where you currently are. Everyone has to start somewhere, but be the woman who can keep her focus on where she wants to be without feeling bad about where she is right now.

"Be thankful for what you have; you'll end up having more. If you concentrate on what you don't have, you will never, ever have enough." —Oprah Winfrey

Prosperous Points

- Your mind is stronger than your body. You have to possess a mind that won't allow your body to give up, even when it seems impossible to keep moving forward.
- Choose to have a good attitude. Life is all about perspective, meaning you have the capability to choose how you react to situations. React positively.
- Never make excuses. Don't train your mind to believe everything is always someone else's fault. Take responsibility for your actions.
- Never say that something is impossible. If you want something bad enough, find a way to make it happen. Like I always say, if you really want something, you'll find a way. If you don't, you'll find an excuse.
- Don't believe the hype. If someone says you're not good enough, don't believe them. If someone says you don't need improvement, don't believe them.
- Be different. God made you an original. Don't die a copy.
- Focus on what you want. Don't give your time and attention to things you don't want. Focus your energy on the things you really want out of life.
- Know your worth. No matter what life throws your way, I promise that you will never lose your value.
- Be grateful for what you have. No matter what the situation, show appreciation. When you can appreciate what you have, you will be given more to appreciate.

Use a Time-Out

(Take time to prioritize your tasks and take care of yourself.)

Let's pretend there is a bank that credits your checking account every day at midnight with $86,400. But there's a catch. You have to spend ALL of the money. Every dime. The balance does not carry over to be used the next day, so if you fail to use it all, the money simply goes to waste.

What would you do if you were a member of this bank? You'd spend all of the money, right? Of course you would! Even if you had to give some of it away to the less fortunate, you'd find a way to put that deposit to good use each and every day. Well, what if I told you that everyone has such a bank? Yes, we all do. It's called time. Every morning, you get 86,400 seconds to spend. If you fail to use the day's deposit, the loss is yours. There is no going back. The balance doesn't carry over to the next day. And any wasted seconds are lost forever.

What does this mean? It means that time is precious. So it's time to start now prioritizing and planning how you will live your best life from here on out. Don't waste anymore time. There's so much value in it.

To realize the value of one year,
ask a student who failed a grade.

To realize the value of one month,
ask a mother who gave birth to a premature baby.

To realize the value of one week,
ask the editor of a weekly newspaper.

To realize the value of one hour,
ask the lovers who are waiting to meet.

To realize the value of one minute,
ask a person who missed the train.

To realize the value of one second,
ask a person who just avoided an accident.

To realize the value of one millisecond,
ask the person who won a silver medal at the Olympics.

As a prosperous woman, you are involved in many different activities for all aspects of your life. Perhaps you are going to school, raising a family, starting a business, playing a sport, advancing your career, and/or volunteering at church. You probably feel as though there isn't enough time in each day. With so many things going on in all aspects of your life, "being busy" is just a natural state of being for you. So what should you do about it?

Make a to-do list. This may seem like simple advice, but it is vital. With a busy schedule, it is easy to forget all that you have to do. So write down everything that you need to get done. Then get to work.

Every time you complete something on your list, take a pen or a highlighter and cross it out. Why? It is psychologically satisfying to see what you have been able to accomplish. In other words, if you have a list of forty-five tasks and you have crossed out thirty-six of them, you will be more motivated to finish the remaining nine, considering the bulk of the work has already been done.

Making to-do lists is a tactic that really works for me. When I don't make a list, I start to feel uneasy about fulfilling all of the things I have to do. When I do make a list, however, I not only feel at ease with having a physical representation of the things I've committed to, but I become excited when I get them done. This may sound a little strange, but trust me, it really works!

Use your time wisely. Having so many things to do is an extremely good reason to use your time wisely. Otherwise, how will you get everything done? I know it can be overwhelming when there are so many things to accomplish. But the key is to prioritize. Ask yourself, "What is the most important thing for me to get done right now?" Then answer the question and do what needs to be done.

If you need to study for an exam, study. If you need to organize your finances, start organizing. If you need to send in your application for graduate school, submit it. If you need to finish a work project, do it. If you need to take your grandmother grocery shopping… okay, you get the picture.

As I said before, we are all given 24-hour days. You, me,

Oprah, Beyoncé. No matter what a person has accomplished in her life, she has been given twenty-four hours in each day just like everyone else. The real question then becomes, "What are you doing with your twenty-four hours?"

Can you honestly say that you are utilizing all twenty-four hours of each day to the best of your ability? Are you doing everything you can to get to where you want to be? Or are you wasting your time with tasks that are getting you nowhere closer to your dreams of prosperity?

If you can't truly say that you are using your time wisely each and every day, then it's time to make a change. Our time on this earth is limited. Every day is a gift and a new chance to make your dreams come true. Don't take your time for granted!

"The essential question is not, 'How busy are you?'
but, 'What are you busy at?'" –Oprah Winfrey

Learn to say no. For some people, it can be a difficult task to say "no." I'm one of those people. I hate to feel like I'm letting someone down. But I've learned that saying "yes" to everything can actually do more harm than good. Think about it. If you're committed to too many things, it's easy to become stressed out. It's easy to work yourself into a panic, wondering how you're going to get everything done. In order to keep your sanity and to accomplish the most important tasks in your life, you have to learn to say no.

If you're anything like me, this will take some practice. But I want you to gain this skill. "No" isn't a bad word. In your case, it's a good word. When you feel like you've committed to too much, just say "no" nicely and move on. If you have to finish your business plan, and your besties want to have a girls' night, all you have to say is, "That sounds like fun, but I really have a lot of work I need to finish up. Let's go next week, and we can do whatever you want to do." In this case, you aren't completely blowing your friends off, just postponing your date. Now, you still get to go out and you won't have to worry about not having fun because you're stressing over your incomplete business plan.

You may be thinking, "Well, I can handle my busy schedule. I don't like telling people no." Or perhaps your thoughts are, "What if I miss out on something?" These thoughts are completely normal. FOMO (fear of missing out) is a real thing. However, at some point, you are going to need some time to spend on yourself. Which brings me to my next point...

Take time to renew yourself. Think of yourself like a car. A car can be driven for miles and miles, but sooner or later, you have to put gas in it if you want to keep driving. As a person, you are the same way. You can't run on empty. You have to find a way to renew your mind, body, and spirit. Whether you choose to go for a drive, do yoga, listen to an inspirational sermon, sleep, watch a funny movie, or hang out with a few friends, you have to renew yourself if you are going to reach your full potential.

MIND

Isn't it hard to think clearly when you have a lot on your plate? Your thoughts seem to be everywhere, which makes it difficult to concentrate on just one thing. I know this feeling all too well. This is why, in renewing yourself, you have to learn how to clear your mind. Rid your brain of worries, to-do lists, past inequities, and unnecessary thoughts so that you can make room for more positive information.

There are plenty of things that you can do to renew your mind. The thing is, I can't tell you what to do. I can only offer suggestions. The process of mind renewal is different for everyone, so you will have to figure out what works for you. Experiment a little, and decide what things you can do on a consistent basis to help you clear and further develop your mind.

For some, it's as simple as picking up a new book to read. For others, a weekend getaway can do the trick. Maybe you'll choose to take a hiatus from social media. Or solve a crossword puzzle. Or watch your favorite movie. Or read your favorite Bible verse. Maybe you'll write in your journal. Or go work out. Or meditate. Maybe you'll go out on a limb and try something you've never tried before. The choice is absolutely yours! The key is to step away from your normal, hectic schedule and clear your mind so that it has the capability of being productive.

Don't make the mistake of thinking that you have to do something drastic and time-consuming to renew your mind and get in a better mental space. The quality of time spent in a renewal state of mind is more important than the quantity. Even just five full minutes of meditation per day can help get you on the right track. We've already established that your mind is a powerful tool. Take care of it! Purge your mind of negativity and open up space for positive interaction.

BODY

Eat right. Get enough sleep. Don't overexert yourself. You've heard all of this before. But it can easily be forgotten, especially when you are determined and traveling on the road to prosperity. Becoming who you are meant to be takes hard work. I know this. But you won't be able to give your best in all aspects of life if you don't take care of your body and give it a chance to recover.

When is the last time you gave your body a break? Have you been working so hard that you haven't been taking care of yourself? If the answer to that last question is "yes," then it's time to take a break. Give your body a chance to renew itself so that you can continue to be productive. Get a massage. Take a bubble bath. Get your hair done. Go to the spa. Pick a day to sleep in. Choose a day when you don't get out of bed. The point is to never beat your body up to the point in which you're actually doing more harm than good. It's okay to take a break from time to time.

When you rest, it recharges your ability to be productive and perform your tasks with the greatest amount of efficiency and energy. Think about how hard it is to accomplish something when you feel completely exhausted and beat down. It's extremely difficult to do anything when you haven't properly slept in days and your body is listless. Help to eliminate this feeling by giving your body a chance to refuel. Allow yourself to become restored.

Now, don't go overboard with your periods of rest! Taking necessary time to renew yourself is very different from lying around and being lazy all day. Remember that even in the creation of the heavens and the earth, God only rested once His work had been done. If He had rested for all seven days, nothing would have been created and we wouldn't be here right now! Like I said before, think of your body like a car. Before you reach empty, you have to put gas in. But once your gas tank is full, you don't keep filling up, do you? Exactly.

Your body is a temple. Treat it that way. As nice as it would be to live 1,000 years with no deterioration to our bodies, life simply doesn't work that way. We are given this body to live on this earth for a limited amount of time. It is imperative that we take care of it in order to carry out our purpose in this lifetime.

> *"When I'm tired, I rest. I say, 'I can't be a superwoman today.'"* –Jada Pinkett Smith

SPIRIT

You know the importance of renewing your mind, and you know the importance of renewing your body. However, sometimes we forget how important it is to renew our spirits.

When everything is going well, it's easy to have a positive outlook on life. When you're well rested both mentally and physically, it's usually not difficult to think clearly. But when you have to walk through a season of adversity, can your spirit withstand the negative blows? When you find yourself in a troubling circumstance, can you maintain the passion to keep walking in your purpose? When you think no one is watching, will you continue to act with integrity?

Your spirit has to be protected. Just like your mind and your body, your spirit has to be renewed. Without consistent revitalization, our spirits can weaken under the pressures of the world. We can begin to feel hopeless in seasons of trials and tribulations. We can start to feel discouraged when things aren't going our way. This is because we were never meant to simply lean on our own earthly understanding. There are things that will happen in our lives, both good and bad, that we will not be able to logically explain. But having a renewed spirit will allow us to reconcile those experiences in our lives.

There are plenty of things you can do to help renew your spirit. Once again, you could meditate. Watch an inspirational movie. Read a spiritual book. Pray. Listen to positive music. Go to church. Pray some more. Talk to your pastor. Even helping another person in her spiritual walk can help you rejuvenate your own. The key is to keep your spirit revitalized and stay connected to the One above.

Stay balanced. When I give speeches at high schools and colleges, one of the most common questions I get from students is, "Did you ever have fun?" I've learned over time to not take offense to this question. Young people just really want to know if it's possible to have fun and still accomplish great things. Well, yes. Yes, it is!

Without balance, you will truly suffer. If your life is all work and no play, you will eventually burn out. And if your life is all play and no work, you will never get anything done. I believe most people understand this concept; however, it can be hard to truly put it into action. It can be hard to say no to friends and fun, even when you know that your education, your career, or your personal goals may be on the line. On the other hand, it can also be hard at times to say no to work, even when you can't remember the last time you've had a break.

When I was in college, my education was my top priority. In particular, I wanted to leave school with a 4.0 GPA, especially since I had never made a B on my report card in elementary, middle, or high school. Although getting good grades was my number one priority, I also knew that it wasn't practical to go through my college career without having any fun. After all, I'm naturally silly, I love to dance, and I thoroughly enjoy sports. I consequently found myself working in the football office, going to parties, and consistently hanging out with my friends. But balance was the key.

Since my grades were my number one priority, mostly everything was scheduled around that; however, I made it a point to add "fun" to my weekly schedules. Because I worked in the football office, it was mandatory I attend every home football game. That was definitely something I never complained about! In addition, my friends and I ate dinner together every day in the dining hall. This may not seem like much, but the time we spent eating dinner was full of jokes, laughter, pranks, and great food. Some of our most memorable moments happened inside of that dining hall. My friends and I still reminisce about those stories to this day!

Then there were the parties. While I was the furthest thing away from a "party girl," I did like to go out and have fun with my friends. But once again, my number one priority was my education. So I made a deal with myself that I would never sacrifice my GPA for a night out. At the same time, I also told myself that if I was caught up with all of my schoolwork, then I wouldn't miss the opportunity to have a little bit of fun.

Obviously I didn't go out with my friends every night of

the week. If I did, I'm pretty sure I wouldn't have been able to maintain my GPA. But the fact remains that I still had a lot of fun. Not only did I accomplish my goal of graduating with a 4.0, I went to dozens of games, attended plenty of parties, shared many laughs with my friends, and truly had the time of my life. My goals were never compromised, and I didn't have to stay locked up in my room to achieve them.

In your own life, make it a point to strive for balance. Don't spend every hour of every day working and forget to recognize the beauty in having a little bit of fun. At the same time, don't get upset that you aren't achieving your goals if you don't want to put in the amount of work necessary to make those goals come to pass.

"No woman can control her destiny if she doesn't give to herself as much as she gives of herself." –Suze Orman

Laugh. It has been said time and time again that laughter is the best medicine. Why? Well, first of all, it helps to relieve stress and pain. It also helps to bring your mind and body into balance by releasing endorphins, the body's natural "feel-good" chemical. Laughter even provides common ground for interacting with other people. In fact, I once heard that laughter is the shortest distance between two people. From my experiences, I believe this to be true.

If you don't believe in the power of laughter, do a quick Internet search to discover the countless stories of people who have used laughter to help heal diseases. Years ago, I heard a story that particularly struck me. It detailed the life of a woman who had been healthy all of her life. When she got to be in her 40s, however, she was given news that she had a large tumor in her chest. The doctors gave her different options, but she decided she would take care of the disease on her own. She went to her local video store and rented hundreds of comedy DVDs. Every day, she watched them, one after the other. She laughed and laughed all day long, until it was time for her to go to bed. The woman did this for months, and when she returned to the doctors they were stunned. The tumor had shrunk, and it was now almost undetectable! This woman literally used laughter to heal herself. That's amazing!

Now, am I saying that laughter should be used as an alternative to modern medicine? No, I'm not. But what I am saying is that laughter has many benefits, and you should make it a point to get your laugh on as often as you can. I mean, why not?

"WHY SO SERIOUS?"

Zack, a Pittsburgh Steelers fan, won a 50-yard-line ticket to see his team play in the Super Bowl. Right before the game was about to start, Zack asked the woman sitting beside him about the empty seat on the other side of her.

"Who in their right mind would have a seat like this and not use it?"

The woman replied, "Well, actually that's my husband's seat. We were supposed to come here together, but he passed away."

"Oh, I'm sorry to hear that! But was there no one you could give the ticket to? A friend? Or a relative?"

The woman shook her head and replied, "No. They're all at the funeral."

When I die, I want to go peacefully in my sleep like my grandfather…not screaming and yelling like the passengers in his car.

Patient: Oh, Doc! I'm just so nervous. This is my very first operation, ever!

Doctor: Don't worry! Mine too!

A nice old lady on a bus offers the driver some peanuts. He's happy to take some, but he asks her after a while why she isn't having any for herself.

"Oh, young man," she says, "they're too hard on my poor teeth. I couldn't."

"Why did you buy them at all then?" asks the driver.

"Because! I just love the chocolate they're covered in!"

A hysterically sounding man calls 911 and yells, "Please come quickly! Miranda is pregnant, and her labor just started! It's really intense!"

"Is this her first child?" asks the operator.

"No, you fool! This is her husband!"

Today, I ran from a ticket inspector. He chased me through half the train. When he finally caught me, he wasn't very amused that I actually did have a ticket.

***

I got a really cute dog and called him Threemiles. It sounds great to say I walk Threemiles twice a day.

***

A guy asks his neighbor in an apartment building: "Mr. Trepper, you live directly above me and you have the same two-room apartment as I do. How many rolls of wallpaper did you buy when you moved in?

"We got eighteen rolls," answers the neighbor.

About a month later, the guy meets his neighbor again and says, "It's really funny – I put the wallpaper up everywhere, and I still had ten rolls left over."

The neighbor smiles, "Yeah, so did we."

Prosperous Points

- Make a "to-do" list. When you accomplish something, cross it out!
- Use your time wisely. Ask yourself, "What is the most important thing for me to get done right now?" When you have that question answered, do whatever needs to be done.
- Learn to say no, because you can't say yes to everything. Don't think "no" is a bad word. When you feel like you've committed to too much, just say "no" nicely and move on.
- Take time to renew your mind, body, and spirit. Think of yourself like a car. A car can be driven for miles and miles, but sooner or later, you have to put gas in it if you want to keep driving.
- Stay balanced. If your life is all work and no play, you will eventually burn out. And if your life is all play and no work, you will never get anything done.
- Laugh! Stop taking everything so seriously.

CUT YOUR LOSSES
(Remove yourself from negative people and situations.)

Every Sunday morning, April takes a light jog around a park near her home. There's a lake located in one corner of the park, and each time April jogs by the lake, she sees the same elderly woman sitting at the water's edge with a small metal cage sitting beside her.

Last Sunday, April's curiosity got the best of her. She stopped jogging and walked over to the elderly lady. As April got closer, she realized that the metal cage was actually a small trap. There were three turtles, unharmed, slowly walking around the base of the trap. The older woman had a fourth turtle in her lap that she was carefully scrubbing with a spongy brush.

"Hello," April said. "I see you here every Sunday morning. If you don't mind me being nosey, I'd love to know what you're doing with these turtles."

The lady smiled. "I'm cleaning off their shells," she replied. "Anything on a turtle's shell, like algae or scum, reduces the turtle's ability to absorb heat and impedes its ability to swim. It can also corrode and weaken the shell over time."

"Wow! That's really nice of you!" April exclaimed.

"Yes, I spend a couple of hours each Sunday morning, relaxing by this lake and helping these little guys out. It's my own weird way of making a difference."

"But don't most freshwater turtles live their whole lives with algae and scum hanging from their shells?" April asked.

"Yes, sadly, they do," the elderly lady replied.

April scratched her head. "Well then, don't you think your time could be better spent? I mean, I think your efforts are kind and all, but there are fresh water turtles living in lakes all around the world. And 99% of these turtles don't have nice people like you to help them clean off their shells. So, no offense, but how exactly are you *truly* making a difference?"

The woman giggled aloud. She then looked down at the turtle in her lap, scrubbed off the last piece of algae from its shell, and said, "Sweetie, if this little guy could talk, he'd tell you I just made all the difference in the world."

This story is the perfect example of how a small act of kindness can truly impact another person's life. In this lifetime, you want to do your best to make sure that your actions are positively influencing others, and that you keep people around you who can positively influence you. In keeping with this positivity, you have to learn to remove yourself from negative people and situations. This will undeniably help propel you on your journey to success.

Not everyone is your friend. I love the analogy that compares the people in your life to the different parts of a tree. You have your leaves, your branches, and your roots. Your leaves are unstable. One day they blow left. One day they blow right, and sometimes they even blow away. When you're up, everything is great, and when you're down, these people are nowhere to be found. Most people in your life are like this.

Then you have your branches. They'll fool you. You think they're all strong and mighty, but as soon as a strong storm comes through, they leave you high and dry. Finally, you have your roots on that tree. These are the people who are there for you through the thick and the thin. Storms may come, but they hold you down. You may be lucky to find three or four "roots" in your entire lifetime. The key in life is distinguishing your leaves from your branches and your roots.

Never make the mistake of confusing people who are always around with people who are genuinely always there for you! Sometimes, we get really messed up trying to put lifetime expectations on people who should only be in our lives for a season. Some people come into our lives for a reason, some for a season, and some for a lifetime. It is absolutely okay if you meet someone who is only supposed to teach you one thing. Learn the lesson, and move on! It's not always necessary to hold on to a relationship just because you two had one great moment, or one great season.

Everyone is not supposed to get to the finish line with you, and that is perfectly fine. Every person you meet does not mean you well, and there are many people who could care less if you succeed. Remember that a lot of people want to see you do better, but they don't necessarily want to see you do better than them. Of course, not all people are like that. You will find people in your life who genuinely want the best for you, and you should hold on to those people. All others, however, you can love at a distance.

Don't give in to negative peer pressure. No one can make you do anything. You may be highly persuaded to take one action over another, but you always have a choice, no matter how hard that choice may seem. Even if someone has you at gunpoint, they can't "make" you do what they say. They can, of course, greatly influence your choices, but they are not in control of your body. Friends work the same way. They can influence your choices, but they can't make them for you.

In order to stay resistant against negative peer pressure, you have to know your own values, goals, and beliefs. You have to know what you stand for, and what you absolutely will not tolerate. When you know these things, you can make better decisions for *yourself*, not for other people.

Think about how each decision you make will affect your future. How would a bad grade affect your chances of getting into your dream graduate program? How would infidelity affect your family dynamic? How would disappointing your child affect his/her outlook on life? How could a negative social media post affect your chances of getting your dream job? Imagine that life is a field of white snow. You have to be careful how you walk this field, because literally every step will show. Decisions you make now will have an effect on your future, whether positive or negative. Make the right decisions today, and be rewarded for it later on in life.

Not all peer pressure is bad. The words "peer pressure" have a negative connotation; however, it is important to realize that not all influence from peers and colleagues has to be bad. Some of this influence can be positive.

There are people in this world who will bring out the best in you. Whether you recognize them or not, you have colleagues, family members, and friends who know what they want out of life and are willing to uplift you on their journey to success. Don't disregard these people. Take advantage of opportunities to continually better yourself. Allow people to influence you optimistically to make you a better person in all aspects of your life. Welcome people into your space who pressure you to do positive things and who believe in your potential. Those are the individuals who will help you grow into the person you are meant to be. Appreciate those people.

Be your own person. You have to know who you are before you can be in a relationship with someone else. And I don't just mean romantic relationships. I also mean friendships. No matter what relationship you have with another person, you should always remain true to yourself. You should never have to change the essence of who you are in order to be someone's friend. Whenever you have a true friend, you can be yourself with that person, flaws and all.

If you find that your "friends" are constantly putting you down, it's time to find new ones. People like this do not care about your feelings and can be damaging to your self-esteem, whether you admit to it or not. If you find that you are trying too hard to keep up an image around your so-called friends, perhaps it's time to evaluate. Are the people around you refusing to accept who you truly are because they would rather be associated with the person you are pretending to be? Or, would those same people accept you regardless? These are important questions to answer, because it is harmful to your well-being to constantly try to be someone else. You may even begin to ask yourself, "Am I good enough?" To answer that question, you *are* good enough! In fact, you are more than good. You are absolutely amazing! Everyone may not be able to appreciate how amazing you are, but those people in your life who really matter will welcome the true you. I think Dr. Seuss said it best when he once stated, "Be who you are and say what you feel, because those who mind don't matter and those who matter don't mind."

Keep in mind that although I said you should avoid those people who try to change the essence of who you truly are, I did not say that you should pursue a group of friends who agree with everything you say. There's a difference. You want people around you who will help you grow and let you know when you are wrong, while still appreciating the person you are today. Don't mistake a friend challenging you with wanting to change you. For example, if all of your friends say that you complain a lot and have a negative outlook on every situation, then perhaps there's truth to that observation. Instead of running away from that group of people for trying to "change" you, take their words as constructive criticism and use it as an opportunity for reflection and growth.

When someone is trying to change you, they don't want to see you grow. They simply want you to be the person they want you to be. They may discredit your job, your goals, your values, your style. They may often put you down and even get mad if you don't conform to their beliefs. This is when you have to make the conscience choice to be your own person.

In all of your relationships, embrace your differences and refrain from comparing yourself to anyone else. You are unique, and you should never try to be someone else in order to be accepted. Whether you're tall, short, skinny, muscular, black, white, purple, or whatever, always make the choice to look at yourself in a positive light. Utilize your personal strengths to achieve your goals. Your strengths will be different from others' strengths, and that is okay! God made you who you are for a reason. Never wish you were different. To wish to be someone else is a waste of the person you truly are. Be you!

> *"Normal is not something to aspire to. It's
> something to get away from."* -Jodie Foster

Know that people change. Next week, your best friend could be your enemy; next year, your enemy could be your best friend. Just remember that the word "change" shouldn't always be associated with something bad. Some individuals around you may change for the worse, just as some may change for the better. Most importantly, are *you* making positive changes in your own life? Are you noticing strides in your personal growth journey? Or are you still the same person that you were last year?

When you find yourself growing in various aspects of your life, you may also discover that you and your friends are heading in two very different directions. Does this mean that you have to completely cut these people out of your life? Not necessarily! But it does likely mean that you may have to love them at a distance.

I have a childhood friend who began to go down a dark path in her late teens. As much as I tried to encourage her and be a positive influence in her life, she continued down this negative path into her twenties. Every interaction I had with her became negative and draining. She attempted to influence me to do things I wouldn't otherwise do, and she developed an awful reputation around the community for her bad behavior. I knew that our relationship couldn't remain the same.

While I didn't completely cut her out of my life, I did have a long talk with her about how her behavior wasn't in alignment with the things I wanted to do in my life. I assured her that I would be there if she ever needed me, and I still reach out to her occasionally to see how she's doing and to offer her words of encouragement. Although I have known her nearly all my life, I also realized that our relationship would become detrimental to my values, beliefs, and future goals if I didn't make a change. It was hard, but I had to accept that she wasn't the person she was early on in our relationship and that loving her at a distance was the best solution moving forward.

By the same token, I have seen individuals with dark pasts grow into the most understanding, loving, and wise people you'd ever want to meet. Just as you have to be able to recognize when a person changes for the worse and must be loved from a distance, you must also be able to identify and appreciate when a person changes for the better. We are all sinners, and we all make mistakes. Don't participate in allowing a person's past to hold them hostage. Don't miss out on the opportunity to build a great relationship with someone simply because you know about a few negative things in their past.

Every so often, take the time to evaluate your relationships with your friends and colleagues. Are you and the people in your circle heading in the same positive direction? Do your friends truly want the best for you? Are you bringing out the best in the people around you? Or are the people you're surrounding yourself with bringing out the worst in you? Answer these questions honestly, so that you can stay on track regarding the people you choose to keep in your life. The quality of your life is directly related to the quality of your relationships. Never forget that.

Teach people how to treat you. The way you choose to treat yourself and others sets the standard for how other people should treat you. If you want other individuals to think highly of you, first think highly of yourself. If you want to be respected, consciously respect yourself and others. If you want your relationship to last, treat your significant other the way you would like to be treated.

When you walk down the street, choose to walk with your head up. When you have a conversation, look people in their eyes. When someone is trying to tell you something, take the time to listen. Why? When people interact with you, they respond to your actions. If you proceed with confidence, you'll be treated like a confident person. If you treat your body with respect, others will be inclined to do the same. Now, of course, you can never control the actions of other people no matter what you do. So I'm not saying that everyone will treat you perfectly just because you put out great vibes and you want them to. But I am saying that the way you act does influence how people treat you.

Just as you can inspire positive behavior, you can also encourage negative behavior. If you're untrustworthy, obviously people will treat you as though you can't be relied upon. If you disrespect yourself and others, other people will think it's okay to disrespect you. It works both ways. So make sure you are always setting a high standard when it comes to teaching people how to treat you.

Don't accept anything less than what you deserve. If someone isn't treating you right, don't let him or her think that it's okay. If you're in a relationship with someone who is constantly putting you down, don't brush it off like it's not a big deal. Let them know that you will not put up with being spoken to in a negative manner. If someone thinks it's okay to treat you in an undesirable manner, they will keep doing it. If that same person knows you will not put up with that kind of treatment, they will refrain from doing it. Think about this in how you personally treat people. You know that there are certain individuals in your life who will allow you to get away with certain things, just as there are people who would never let you live it down if you behaved in a certain way. You know the people you can "try" and those you can't.

What do the people in your life think about you? Do they think that you will accept negative behavior? Or do they know that you have tall standards regarding the people you keep around and how you will allow them to treat you? Answer these questions honestly, and make adjustments when necessary. Always, always, always set the bar high when it comes to teaching people how you should be treated. You deserve it.

See the world. Whether you can afford to actually travel around the world is irrelevant. You don't need to be a world traveler to unlock your potential. What you do need, however, is to be open to new experiences. That's what I mean when I say to "see the world." You can't spend your entire life inside your own comfort zone. You cannot grow like that.

When is the last time you spoke to someone from a completely different background? Have you ever taken the time to sit down and talk to your friends about their personal and professional goals? If you've been "privileged" all of your life, when is the last time you've spent time in a poorer neighborhood or volunteering in an environment where most people have less than you? If you've never been afforded the finer things in life, have you ever taken a drive through a neighborhood of people where money is the least of their worries? When is the last time you've been outside of your community?

The world is a classroom. There is always an opportunity to learn, to see new things, to have new experiences. Never miss out on the chance to see more than what is constantly around you. You must use these experiences to help you grow into a well-rounded individual who has more than just one perspective on life. Your prosperity depends on it.

Build positive relationships. You've heard the saying before: "It's not what you know. It's who you know." While this saying is often used to emphasize the importance of networking in achieving career goals, I like to apply it to life in general. Your existence isn't solely about achievement. After all, how enjoyable is success if there is no one with whom to share it? Life is also about building relationships with others who can pour into you as you pour into them. As I said before, the quality of your life is often equivalent to the quality of your relationships. Are you putting forth the effort to build strong, genuine connections with people who impact your well-being, and will continue to?

If you're going through some struggles in life, whom can you call? If you need a reference or letter of recommendation, whom can you depend on? Who do you trust enough to share your goals with? Who would you reach out to if you needed to "get away?" If you want to start a business venture, whom could you count on to give you sound advice?

The mistake that many people make when building relationships is that they are not genuinely trying to connect with the other person. They are simply trying to see what they can get. Never pursue a relationship with the intent of trying to use another person. Relationships grow when they are mutually beneficial; consequently, your goal should never be to see what you can obtain from another person. Instead, you should always see how you can serve that individual. If they enter the relationship with the same mindset, then you can progress accordingly. You can grow to have each other's backs, help each other when needed, provide appropriate introductions, and offer emotional support. But no one wants to feel like they're in a relationship with a "taker." And if all you're doing is befriending people for your own benefit, then you will be seen as doing just that.

Relationships take work, whether they're romantic or platonic. In order to build a positive connection, both of you have to pour into each other. Just as you should not allow yourself to become a taker in any relationship, you should also evaluate associations in which others are constantly taking from you. Do you always perform favors for others with no appreciation? Are you always there for people who aren't there for you? Is there an individual in your life who is forever draining?

As you continue to go through life, the importance of

building positive relationships will become more and more evident. Life isn't all about how much you know or what you have accomplished. It's about the connections you have with other people, and the mutual positivity that results from it.

Optimistically impact other people's lives. This point is short, because it is very straightforward. Just as others can help to bring out the best in you, you want to make sure you are bringing out the best in other people. Encourage your friends. Be happy for others. Smile. Volunteer. Pay it forward whenever you can. Understand that the world does not revolve around you. So take the time to do things that aren't solely beneficial to your own life. Consistently serve other people, and consciously be a light in the world by impacting others' lives.

"The most common way people give up their power is by thinking they don't have any." –Alice Walker

Prosperous Points

- Not everyone is your friend. Be able to recognize the people who have your best interest in mind.
- Don't give in to negative peer pressure. Think about how each decision you make will affect your future.
- Not all peer pressure is bad. There are individuals who will help you grow into the person you are meant to be. Appreciate those people.
- Be your own person. You have to know who you are before you can be in a relationship with someone else. Never wish you were different. To wish to be someone else is a waste of the person you truly are.
- Know that people change. Next week, your best friend could be your enemy; next year, your enemy could be your best friend. Take time to evaluate and make sure that the people in your life are leading you in a positive direction.
- Teach people how to treat you. The way you choose to treat yourself and others sets the standard for how other people should treat you.
- See the world. Be open to new experiences. There is always an opportunity to learn and see new things.
- Build positive relationships. Life isn't all about how much you know or what you have accomplished. It's about the relationships you have with other people, and the mutual positivity that results from these relationships.
- Optimistically impact other people's lives. Benefit others and be a positive light in someone else's life.

GO BACK TO SQUARE ONE
(Learn from failure, and start anew.)

During an impressive research experiment, Linda, a marine biologist, placed a shark into a large holding tank. After giving the shark a chance to swim around, Linda released several small baitfish into the tank. As you would expect, the shark quickly attacked and ate the smaller fish.

Linda then inserted a strong piece of clear fiberglass into the tank, creating two separate partitions. She put the shark on one side of the fiberglass and a new set of baitfish on the other. Again, the shark quickly attacked. This time, however, the shark slammed into the fiberglass divider. Unfazed, the shark kept trying to attack the fish. Meanwhile, the baitfish swam around unharmed in the second partition. After about an hour into the experiment, the shark just gave up.

Over the next few weeks, this experiment was repeated several dozen times. Each time, the shark got less aggressive and made fewer attempts to attack the bait fish, until eventually the shark got tired of slamming into the fiberglass and simply stopped attacking altogether.

After noticing the shark's defeat, Linda removed the

fiberglass divider before performing the experiment again. She proceeded to add the baitfish; however, the shark didn't attack. The shark was trained to believe that a barrier still existed, so the baitfish swam wherever they wished, completely free from harm. The shark, of course, could have attacked and eaten the fish at any time. But because it thought a barrier existed, the shark was stuck right where it was.

Like this shark, how many of us go through life thinking we cannot do something, simply because we failed at it a few times before? I'm here to tell you that if you want to be prosperous, you cannot have this mentality. If you fall down, stand back up, carrying with you the lessons from that fall.

Pay attention to your mistakes. There is an old proverb that states, "Don't look at where you fell. Look at where you tripped." This means that with any failure, you have to pinpoint the *actual* problem so that you can work to correct it. It's easy to place the blame on other people and situations when things don't go our way, but a wise person taught me a long time ago that truly successful people always take less of their share of the credit and more of their share of the blame. Instead of looking at everyone and everything else as the cause for your setback, ask yourself what you could have done differently to get a different outcome.

Was the test really too hard, or did you not study hard enough? Was the competition really too tough, or did you not prepare adequately? Is your spouse complaining for no reason, or could you make a better effort in your communication?

I remember when I got to college and failed my first test (in that difficult economics class I told you about). I distinctly recall being absolutely devastated when I got my grade back. Keep in mind that I was a 16-year-old college sophomore who had graduated valedictorian from my high school. I had never even gotten a B on my report card! Now, I had failed a test?!

My first reaction to my shortcoming was to come up with excuses. "Everyone else failed." "This professor isn't very good." "The stuff on the test wasn't even in our notes!" "Maybe I should just drop this class."

Despite each excuse I tried to make, the truth was that I could have done more to make sure I was prepared for the exam. Yes, everyone else failed that first test. Yes, many students in the class complained about the professor. Yes, there were things on the test that we didn't thoroughly go over. But the fact remained that I needed that class for graduation, and my first mistake started with me thinking that I wouldn't have to put an enormous amount of effort into that economics class (which everyone had previously told me was a difficult class to pass). To be completely honest, I didn't think I would have to put too much effort into *any* class. Despite previously attending a nationally ranked high school, I never had a class in which I struggled.

In order to find success in my college economics class, I first had to recognize my mistake of not putting forth the effort necessary to get an A. In all actuality, I was overly confident, and I realized that I needed to do more. Otherwise, my misunderstanding of key concepts would have led me in a downward spiral from which I may not have been able to recover.

Once I realized my true mistake, it was time for me to make a plan. I started by giving the professor 100% of my attention during each and every class. I emailed him regularly about assignments. I visited him during his office hours to go over homework problems. Instead of trying to figure things out on my own, I asked questions whenever I was unsure of a concept. I read all corresponding chapters in the book, taking my own notes in addition to the ones he gave us. I did everything I possibly could to make sure that I was successful in that class.

When the second exam rolled around, I was much more prepared. I not only received an A, but I was the only student to get a 100. By the time the end of the semester came, I had the highest average in the class and was told that I could exempt the final exam!

As I said before, I didn't end with the highest grade in the class because I was smarter than anyone else. I worked my butt off! But before I could begin with the hard work, I had to be realistic about my mistakes and avoid making excuses.

Falling short should never be seen as a bad thing. Making mistakes is okay! As you can see, failing that first exam didn't keep me from getting my desired grade in that class. But never make a mistake without taking the time to reflect and learn from the experience. Because once you know why you tripped, you can prevent many future falls.

> "If you don't like the road you're walking, start
> paving another one." –Dolly Parton

Allow failure to teach you. One of my favorite quotes belongs to Michael Jordan. When once talking about all of his success, he once stated, "In my career, I've missed over 9,000 shots. I lost over 300 games. Twenty-six times, I've been trusted to take the game-winning shot and I missed. I've failed over and over and over again in my life. That is why I succeed."

Is that powerful, or what? Michael Jordan is often considered to be the best person to ever play the sport of basketball. A self-made billionaire, he has accomplished more than many can even imagine. However, even with all of his success, he knows that his failures are what allowed him to achieve such a high level of greatness.

Whether you fail a big test, bomb the interview, get overlooked for your dream job, or make a mistake that ruins a relationship, never allow your situation to defeat you. You have to get back up and keep moving forward. Think about it this way. No matter what you have gone through, you're still here, so there is still purpose in your life! Despite your failures and shortcomings, there are still things for you to accomplish. Learn from your setbacks and keep moving forward in a positive direction.

Let's go back for a quick moment to my sophomore year of college, during which I was taking that stressful economics class. At the time, it wasn't good enough that I recognized my mistake at the beginning of the semester. I had to take it a step further. I had to recognize the mistake and then *learn* from it. I had to not only formulate a plan to get through the rest of the semester successfully, but I also had to remember the lesson I previously learned at the beginning of each subsequent semester when I started a new class.

Experiencing failure and suffering obstacles on your journey doesn't only allow you to learn and grow, but it also allows you to fully appreciate when you do achieve your goal. I can tell you one thing. Of all the As I received on my college transcript, the A beside that particular economics class is one that I'm most proud of. When I remember the blood, sweat, and tears that accompanied my journey to that A, it makes me proud and appreciative of the final results.

It's often hard to see at the time, but there are multiple benefits to failure. It builds our grit, and it allows us to further appreciate when we achieve our goals. Beyond these benefits, failure has a simple function at its core. It is meant to teach us so that we won't make the same mistakes again. By looking at our past situations, we can discern the actions we must take to achieve prosperity in all aspects of our lives.

Appreciate the little things. Many times, failure teaches us to appreciate the little things in life. Think about it. When things are going along great, it's easy to take the things and people around us for granted. But when we are in a struggle, we realize how important the "little things" are. If you and your best friend aren't on speaking terms, you start to appreciate the friendship you once had. If you get sick, you may recognize that you've been taking your health for granted. If you're going through a rough season with your spouse, you value the previous peace you had within your home. If someone in your family passes away, you may regret not showing them how much you really cared. If you are experiencing unexpected financial difficulty, you realize the importance of saving and making smart financial decisions.

Don't wait for tragedy to unearth your appreciation for the people and things around you. Take time each day to show your gratitude. If you have a roof over your head, be grateful. If you have food to eat, be thankful. If you have people in your life who love you, show appreciation. If you have the ability to speak, only say kind words. If you have breath in your body, continue to take care of your temple. Never take people or situations for granted!

There once was a young lady named Jordyn who was in her first year of medical school. She had always been an A student, and she was similarly excelling in all of her classes at the university where she was studying medicine. In one particular class, the professor gave the students a quiz every Friday, consisting of ten questions. Jordyn always did well, so she was a bit surprised to see a question on one particular quiz that seemed to have nothing to do with the material they had been studying in class.

The tenth question on the quiz read as follows: "What is the first name of the lady who cleans up this building?" Jordyn looked around the classroom at her other classmates, who also looked confused. How were they supposed to know that? Sure, the cleaning lady was always sweet, but how were they supposed to know her name? One of her classmates boldly raised his hand to ask a question.

"Professor! Will this last question count toward our grade?"

The professor looked around at all of the students who were wondering the same thing. She replied,

"Of course it will count. In your careers, you're going to meet a lot of different people, and you're going to have a lot of different experiences. But you can never pass off anything as unimportant. Some of you seem to take for granted that this building is always clean. Perhaps you should give thanks to the woman who is responsible for that."

Jordyn went back to her apartment and thought about

what her professor said. As important as it was for her to study and finish all of her assignments, she realized that she also needed to take some time to just smell the roses. Jordyn never did forget that lesson. She also learned the name of the woman who cleaned up the building was Dorothy.

This story demonstrates the importance of taking the time to recognize and appreciate the positive forces around us, no matter how small or insignificant they may seem on the surface. Yes, Jordyn and her classmates were studying to be doctors. Yes, their main focus was on mastering the required material so that they could move on to complete their residencies. But Dorothy was always in the building. She cleaned up after them, and kept the building neat. She was always pleasant, no matter what time of day. So, why not greet her by name? Why not show her some appreciation with a smile, a "thank you," or a simple "hello"?

In your own life, always make a conscious effort to recognize all of the beauty around you, and try your best to appreciate the little things. When things are going along well, be thankful. And even when things aren't that great, also be thankful. No matter how bad things may seem, they could always be worse. You can always find something for which to be appreciative no matter what the situation may be. Whether you thank the Lord above for the service workers in your industry, or for the breath that's still in your body, find something for which to be grateful and never take anything for granted.

Learn from others. Don't think that the only way you can learn is by making your own mistakes. Learn from others as well. There's a proverb that says, "A wise woman learns from the mistakes of others, a fool by her own." If you look at the lives of other people and observe what did (or didn't) work for them, use them as examples. Use other individuals' stories of success and failure to give you an idea of the general path you should be on.

The reason why I always read books and business magazines is because I personally love reading about individuals' paths to success. What's even better than reading is actually getting the opportunity to pick people's brains about their personal journeys. No matter how successful a person is, he or she has made mistakes and has experienced setbacks. The overcoming of those obstacles breeds great wisdom that is often readily shared with those willing to listen and learn.

The next time you have the opportunity to learn from another prosperous woman, don't hesitate to do so. Absorb how those women have navigated the waters to get to where they are today, and take notes! Where did they stumble? How can you avoid their mistakes? How can you do things differently? What were some of the best decisions they made? There's power in knowledge. Never miss the chance to expand your knowledge by studying the experiences of other successful people.

"Learn from the mistakes of others. You can't live long enough to make them all yourself." –Eleanor Roosevelt

Start fresh. Every day is a new day, so don't dwell on the mistakes of yesterday. No matter how many times you have fallen down before, have a positive mentality as you set out to achieve your goals. Get back up with a renewed mindset and keep on going.

Never allow the negativity of your past to determine your future. Now, I know that sometimes it can be hard to get back up after we are really knocked down. And it's okay to be upset. It's okay to cry. It's okay to be angry. After you release your frustrations, however, you must make a conscious effort to keep moving forward with your aspirations, despite what may have happened.

If you decide to give your relationship another chance after experiencing some type of pain, you have to intentionally remind yourself that you have forgiven the other person and that you are willing to move forward with no reference to the previous situation. You cannot walk through the door of greatness with one foot still outside in the past. Starting fresh means STARTING FRESH. Go to counseling, pray together, spend lots of time in church. But don't keep torturing yourself with details of the past that will prevent you from truly moving forward.

If you failed your Bar exam, don't go into your next exam still thinking about the time before when you failed. Use your previous experience to better prepare for the next test. Build your confidence, and don't sign up for another exam until you are sure of your ability to do well. After your preparation has been completed, walk into your next Bar examination with the confidence that you are going to do better than before.

There are so many situations in life when we have to pick ourselves back up. Whether it's an unsuccessful relationship, a failed test, a health scare, an injury, a miscarriage, or a family crisis, you will be okay! You will get through it! And when you pick yourself up, do so with a renewed mind that will allow you to keep moving forward toward your destiny.

My life is nowhere near perfect. I've been in multiple situations in which I wanted to quit, in which I wanted to completely break down. But I didn't. I cried my tears to cleanse my soul and I realized the bigger plan God had for me. I realized that I had to use what I'd gone through to propel me to a greater level of success. To this day, whenever I find myself wanting to dwell in the past, I think about one of my favorite quotes: "Look at life through the windshield. Not the rearview mirror." We will have setbacks. We are only human. But after every failure, we have to pick ourselves up and start fresh, looking forward to the beauty of our dreams.

Prosperous Points

- Pay attention to your mistakes. There is an old proverb that states, "Don't look at where you fell. Look at where you tripped." Pinpoint the *actual* problem so that you can work to correct it.
- Allow failure to teach you. Use the situation to learn what to do (or not do) next time.
- Appreciate the little things. Never pass off blessings in life as unimportant. If you find yourself in a struggle and you start to feel ungrateful, find something to be thankful for. Things could always be worse.
- Learn from others. Don't think that the only way you can learn is by making your own mistakes. There's a proverb that says, "A wise woman learns from the mistakes of others, a fool by her own."
- Start fresh. Don't dwell in the past. If you make a mistake, learn from it and move on. "Look at life through the windshield, not the rearview mirror."

NEVER THROW IN THE TOWEL

(Never, ever, ever give up!)

A young girl was playing outside when she found a co-coon of a butterfly. Each day, the girl checked on the cocoon, hoping to see the butterfly emerge. One day, a small opening appeared. She sat and watched the butterfly struggle to force its body through that little hole. It seemed as if the butterfly had stopped making any progress. In fact, the butterfly looked stuck.

Concerned, the girl decided to help the butterfly. She took a pair of scissors and snipped the cocoon to make the hole bigger. Before long, the butterfly broke free! The young girl was surprised, however, to see that the butterfly had a swollen body and small, shriveled wings. She continued to watch the butterfly, thinking that the body would shrink and the wings would expand. But that didn't happen.

The butterfly spent the rest of its life unable to fly, crawling around with tiny wings and a swollen body. Despite the kind heart of the young girl, she didn't understand that the restricting cocoon and the butterfly's struggle to get itself through the small opening were God's way of forcing fluid from the body of the butterfly into its wings to prepare itself for flying once it was out of the cocoon.

As with the butterfly attempting to escape from the cocoon, adversity often presents itself in our lives. Most often, difficulties seem to come at the worst times. But adversity serves a purpose. Hardships are not meant to break us. On the contrary, our struggles in life are meant to help develop our strengths so that we can spread our wings and fly.

Push through adversity. Use difficult circumstances to teach you, not defeat you. No matter how hard things may seem, make a conscious decision to never give up. You are closer to achieving your goals than you think. In fact, most of life's greatest misfortunes are represented by people who gave up, not realizing how close to success they actually were.

Can you imagine having twenty-two brothers and sisters? You probably wouldn't get much attention. What if you got the attention you wanted, but only because you were a very sick child? You suffered from the measles, scarlet fever, double pneumonia, and polio, a disease with no cure. For years, you were forced to walk with metal leg braces and were told that you would never be an athlete. Despite suffering all of this as a child, you never give up. You become the first American woman to win three gold medals in track and field during a single Olympic Games at the 1960 Rome Olympics. That's exactly what Wilma Rudolph did.

What if your only goal was to become a professional figure skater? You work hard for your entire life, doing everything it takes in order to make the Olympic team. Despite all of your dedication, hard work, and perseverance, you fail to make the Olympics. You decide to completely shelve your skating career and take a job in retail. Despite walking away from your original dream, you bust your butt in this new arena of your life. You go from Yves Saint Laurent Boutique in New York City to *Vogue* in just two years, eventually becoming one of the world's most visible fashion designers. Known internationally for her signature bridal gowns, Vera Wang didn't let an unfulfilled dream keep her from accomplishing many more.

When is the last time you truly took a stand for what is right? What if you decided to fight for civil rights during a time when segregation was still legal and racism was at an all-time high? You take a stand against racial inequality and refuse to give up your bus seat to a white man in Montgomery, Alabama. What if, in the midst of trying to do the right thing, you lose your job and receive death threats? Would you keep up the fight? Rosa Parks did. She remained an active member of the NAACP, and in 1999 she received the Congressional Gold Medal of Honor, the highest honor a civilian can receive in the United States.

Imagine being tormented at the thought of going to school because the bullying you experience is so extreme. Despite being bullied, you maintain the drive to create music. As a child, you take voice lessons and learn to play classical piano. You get accepted to NYU Tisch School of Arts, but you soon drop out to pursue your real-world dreams. You get a record deal at age nineteen, thinking that your success is right around the corner. But around that same period of time, you are raped by someone twenty years older. You tell no one, continuing to focus on your music; however, you are now an independent artist because your record label drops you. You experiment with drugs and suffer from PTSD. Although circumstances try to keep you down, you eventually sign with a new record label. You become the first artist (male or female) in the history of the Billboard's Pop Songs to send her first six singles to number one. You even win multiple Grammy Awards and an Academy Award. You become loved and respected by people around the world due to your empowering vocals and lyrics. Meet Lady Gaga.

"Knowing what must be done does away with fear." –Rosa Parks

AMAZING WOMEN WHO DIDN'T GIVE UP

<u>Kerri Strug</u>: At the 1996 Atlanta Olympics, Strug was a member of the "Magnificent Seven," who won the United States' first women's gymnastics Olympic team gold medal. But she wasn't *just* a member of the team. She was the main reason why they were able to pull off the win. As the last competitor on vault, she had to score a 9.493 in order to secure the United States' gold medal (her teammate fell on the previous turn). As she completed her first vault, however, she fell, scoring a 9.162. Not only did she fail to score high enough to win the gold for her team, she hurt her ankle. Unknown at the time, she had sprained her ankle and torn two ligaments. In spite of the injury, she didn't give up. She limped down the runway to her starting spot and got ready to perform her final vault. She ran back down the runway, flipped over the vault, and landed on one foot. After saluting the judges, she fell to the ground in pain. As she was carried off of the mat, her score appeared. She received a 9.712, which gave the United States the necessary score to win.

Jennifer Hudson: Although she is now an Oscar-winning actress and Grammy-winning singer, Hudson's life hasn't always been a dream. Growing up in a crime-ridden Chicago neighborhood, she always loved to sing. Because of her dream to become a professional singer, Hudson's mother encouraged her to try out for *American Idol*. Although she gained a large fan following, she did not win the show. Disappointed, it wouldn't be long until she would receive the opportunity of a lifetime: She was cast as "Effie White" in *Dreamgirls*, ultimately winning her a Golden Globe and an Academy Award. In the midst of her prestigious award-winning season, she publicly struggled with her weight; however, that would soon become the least of her worries. In 2008, Hudson's world came crashing down with news that her brother, mother, and nephew were all killed by her sister's estranged husband in a home invasion/kidnapping. Despite hitting the lowest of lows, she came back stronger than ever before. Winning two Grammy Awards since that time, she has also been an influential spokesperson for Weightwatchers. In addition, Hudson started the Julian D. King Gift Foundation in her slain nephew's honor. Because of her charity work, she was honored with the Favorite Humanitarian at the People's Choice Awards in 2014.

Monica Seles: Seles is a member of the International Tennis Hall of Fame, formerly ranked number one in the world. In 1993, an obsessed fan ran from the middle of the crowd during a tennis match and stabbed Seles in the back with a 9-inch long knife. After recovering from the incident, she made an astounding comeback, winning the 1996 Australian Open and earning a bronze medal at the 2000 Sydney Olympics.

<u>Kris Carr</u>: After a regular check-up at her doctor's office, Carr was informed that she had a rare and incurable Stage IV cancer called epithelioid hemangioendothelioma, affecting her liver and lungs. Instead of letting the disease negatively impact her life, she decided to use her experiences to inspire people all over the world. She produced a documentary entitled *Crazy Sexy Cancer* and became a New York Times bestselling author of multiple health books. Her goal is to not only provide support to women who have been diagnosed with cancer, but to inspire all people to be positive through adversity and live their best lives.

> "Step out of the history that is holding you back. Step into the new story you are willing to create." –Oprah Winfrey

Stop trying to pray the adversity away. Let's face it. No one has a perfect life. At some point in time, we will all face difficulties, no matter how big or small. In facing this adversity, it is often easy to try to "pray it away." After all, if something is causing you pain, it's best to get rid of it, right?

There is an old proverb that states, "I do not pray for a lighter burden. I pray for a stronger back." From the moment I first heard that quote, I changed the way I choose to view stressful situations. Adversity serves a positive purpose; it is meant to make us better, not bitter. It is meant to be used as a tool to help us grow into the individuals we are meant to be. Let's be real. Without adversity, we would never know what we are truly capable of achieving. At the end of the day, pressure is what creates diamonds.

After pondering that old proverb, it no longer made sense for me to pray for adverse situations in my life to just disappear. It seemed to make more sense for me to ask for the courage to overcome any negativity, learn from the situation, and come out stronger in the end.

There have been many times in my life in which I asked, "Why is this happening to me, God? Can you not give this battle to someone else?" Whether it was a health issue, a death in my family, or a stressful season in my life, I would find myself questioning the purpose for my current struggle. For example, I'll never forget when I was seventeen years old, and I went to the doctor for a normal check-up. I told my doctor about a lump that I had found in my right breast, but I honestly thought that he was going to tell me it was nothing and send me on my way. Instead, he asked me to come to his office and wanted to know if my mom was close by. I texted my mom and told her to come down the street to the doctor's office. Once she got there, my doctor explained that he didn't think the lump in my breast was "nothing," and he wanted to refer me to a breast cancer doctor. *Wait, what?!* Let's not forget that I was only seventeen years old. I could barely drive home. A breast cancer doctor? How could this be? I cried for the rest of the day. Then I decided that I had to be strong.

I went to the appointment with Dr. Young, the breast cancer surgeon. He sent me to get an ultrasound, which showed the growth in my right breast. Although Dr. Young said that he couldn't be sure without a biopsy, he believed the growth was benign; however, we all agreed that it would be best to move forward with surgery. I had the operation, and by the grace of God, the growth was in fact benign. My family and I were beyond happy, and I was ready to move forward with my life. Then about a year and a half later, it happened again.

I am not exactly sure why, but I decided to give myself a breast exam in the shower. After my initial lumpectomy, my doctor told me to occasionally check both of my breasts, but it wasn't at the top of my priority list. After all, I was only nineteen and my previous issue had been resolved. What was the actual likelihood that I would experience that again? Well, I was about to get my answer. I called my doctor, who immediately referred me to Dr. Young again.

"To be completely honest, this one concerns me," said Dr. Young when my mom and I arrived for the appointment. Clearly, those were not the words I wanted to hear. He explained that this growth was bigger than the one before and that it had grown quite fast. He wanted to remove the tumor, as well as additional, healthy surrounding tissue to make sure that nothing else was going on.

This time around, I was beyond nervous. What if this was more than just a benign growth? Why did it come back? Why was it growing so fast? How much healthy tissue would Dr. Young take? Too many thoughts were running through my head. Outwardly, I remained strong. Inwardly, however, I didn't know what to think.

On the day of the surgery, all I could do was pray. I was nervous, and I just couldn't understand why this was happening to me. I just wanted it to all go away. I was rolled into the operating room, and the next thing I knew I was waking up in the recovery wing.

My mom was standing over me with tears in her eyes. *Oh no!* I thought. *It's cancer.*

"It was benign," my mom said, through her tears of joy.

Quickly, I let out sighs of relief. I was going to be okay! But for weeks, I had no idea what the outcome would be. I immediately thanked God, and I realized how much I took for granted. I made up my mind right there that I would make the absolute most of my life, because each day is not promised. Our current living situations aren't promised. Our health isn't promised. The people we love won't always be here. So I pledged to myself that I would do everything I could every day to make sure I live my life to the fullest.

As difficult as that experience was, I know that those two lumpectomies helped to mold me into the person I am today. It forced me to appreciate the true value of life at a young age, and it drove me to want to do my absolute best with the gifts and resources God has given me. After rereading the book of Job during that time, I consciously realized that adversity is a part of life, but if we can past the tests that come our way, we will come out stronger and wiser in the end.

When we learn to embrace adversity, we give ourselves amazing opportunities to grow emotionally, spiritually, and physically. In the midst of a struggle, it is often easy to just break down and give up. However, in reality, hardships are a lot like workouts. Yes, it's painful at the time. But after consistent periods of intense focus, it becomes apparent that you are much stronger than you were before.

Keep the big picture in mind. When we find ourselves in a troubling circumstance, it's easy to lose sight of the big picture.

If you make a C in a class, you may lose sight of the fact that there are twenty As on your transcript. If you and your spouse have been constantly fighting for the past month, you might forget all of the positive experiences you've had together over the years. If you lose two competitions in a row, you may forget that you had eight consecutive wins before that. If you're going through a rough season in your life, you might start to believe that every aspect of your being is bad.

Situations like these can cause you to make decisions that you will later regret. For example, a few bad competitions might cause you to think it's time to quit. A few bad grades may have you contemplating dropping out. A few recent fights might persuade you to end a relationship. A negative season can even produce suicidal thoughts. But you have to look at the big picture, beyond your current struggles. Ask yourself a few questions in each case: Do I really *want* to give up? How would quitting truly affect me? If my situation was better right now, would I even consider walking away? Is this something worth fighting for? How can I look at this from a different perspective? How can I stop hurting without making the ultimate sacrifice?

Sometimes, things get hard. Really hard. I know that. And I've been through rough seasons myself. But you have to remember what you are fighting for. You have to remember your goals, and you can't forget the big picture.

I once heard a quote that went something like this: "When you feel like giving up, remember why you held on so long in the first place." Never, ever give up because of a temporary situation. Things will get better if you just hold on.

"You may encounter many defeats, but you must not be defeated. In fact, it may be necessary to encounter the defeats, so you can know who you are, what you can rise from, how you can still come out of it." –Maya Angelou

Never cut what you can untie. Years ago, I was washing my hair in the sink when I almost killed myself. My hair got tangled in the drain, causing the water level to quickly rise. I couldn't move my head, which made me panic. I screamed for my mom to come help me. She wasn't coming fast enough, so I screamed again. I heard her coming up the stairs, but I felt like she was going to be too late. There was a pair of scissors just barely out of my reach. I knew I had to cut my hair if I was going to survive. I was hardly able to breathe. Just as I got my hand on the scissors, my mom came through the door. "RAVEN!" She stood in the doorway as I brought the scissors closer to my head. "Turn the water off!!" I paused. The water had just begun to cover my face, and I felt like a complete idiot. I reached my hand over my head to turn the water off. After a minute or two, the water finally completely drained from the sink and my mom helped me untangle my hair. I laugh about it now, but that experience truly taught me a lot about life. I was so caught up in the moment of the water rising that I wasn't thinking straight. At all. From that point on, I made the conscious decision to STOP AND THINK anytime I find myself in an emotionally charged circumstance. Whether I'm in a difficult situation, having an argument, in the midst of making an important decision, or washing my hair (laughs), I never want to find myself making a permanent negative decision because of a temporary situation.

My point is this: No matter how hard things may seem. No matter what circumstance you find yourself in. No matter what people tell you. No matter what life throws at you. Never, ever, ever give up!

Listen to God. It doesn't matter how badly we want something. If it is not in God's plan for us, it's not going to happen (or if it does happen, it won't be sustainable). This is why we must learn to listen to God. We must learn to align ourselves with His plans and allow Him to order our steps. That is the only way to truly find prosperity in all aspects of your life.

Sometimes, when we want something so desperately, we ignore God's voice. We get into a frame of mind in which we want what we want, and we don't allow anything to deter us. Don't get me wrong. It's perfectly fine to be determined and persistent. In fact, that tenacity is the only way that you will be able to successfully overcome adversity and achieve any worthwhile dream. However, we have to remember that in order to find success, our actions must align with God's will. So the question then becomes, "How do we align ourselves with His plans for us?"

I don't know about you, but I can't remember the last time God made Himself known to me through a clear, audible voice that echoed from a random, burning bush (shout out to Moses). Instead, God often uses signs that are recognizable as long as we are in tune with Him. Sometimes these signs can come in the form of a "tugging" on our heartstrings. We may begin to feel as though we are being led in a certain direction to perform a particular task, and no matter how hard we try to run away from the feeling, it keeps returning. Sometimes God presents Himself in a dream. Sometimes the exact song you need to hear comes on the radio at the time you need to hear it. Other times, God places people in our lives who speak truth to us and provide advice that is in alignment with His plans. The key is to constantly pray about your decisions and stay open to His will. Most of the time, things happen on our journey that naturally help to steer us in the right direction. We just have to be open to His direction.

When I was younger, I was extremely passionate about gymnastics. By age ten, I was a level ten gymnast (the highest level in the Junior Olympic program), and my goals were set high. Multiple coaches asked me whether college gymnastics was my ultimate goal, or if I wanted to begin taking steps to potentially fulfill an Olympic dream. Not too long after I started making these grand plans, my knees started hurting, and the pain would not go away. I practiced through the pain for months before receiving a diagnosis. I was told I had a severe case of Osgood-Schlatter disease. Although many kids outgrow this condition with time, my doctors warned me that my case was bad, and my gymnastics career would probably take a hit.

Even though I was determined to prove my doctors wrong, my body had other plans. The pain would not subside with ice, ibuprofen, cortisone shots, or physical therapy, and I didn't want to take a break from the sport. How else was I supposed to accomplish my dreams? Other girls on my team had injuries and pain, but no one seemed to have the lingering, chronic pain that I was experiencing.

As time passed, other injuries kept occurring to further keep me down. While performing a release move on bars one night, I hit my head on the bar in a freak accident and cracked my skull. I had a huge knot on my head that was so big, one of my teammates shouted out, "I thought that only happened in cartoons!" Even when the knot finally went down, I still had a constant reminder of my injury: a headache that just wouldn't go away. My doctor told me to forego the first meet of the season. I couldn't believe it. Was God giving me a sign? Why couldn't I catch a break?

When I was finally cleared for practice, I came back at the top of my game. I was still in a lot of pain from my knee disorder, but my coach and I modified my practice schedule, and I did well at every competition. By the end of the season, I had become the youngest person from my state to qualify to the Level 10 Junior Olympic National Championships. I felt on top of the world. At least until it was time to compete at Nationals. My coach didn't come with me because he was scared to fly (I'm from South Carolina, and the meet was in California). Instead, he sent his wife with me, which of course just wasn't the same. I was beyond nervous, and I literally had the most disappointing meet of my life. It was honestly the absolute worst way to end the season.

I felt like I was at a crossroad. I knew I had a God-given ability to do gymnastics, but I couldn't understand my injuries and why I was always in so much pain. I couldn't comprehend how I could make it all the way to the most prestigious competition of the season, just to blow it.

Around this time, I started getting many speaking requests. I had published my first book just months before, so I was being invited to speak to youth groups and schools all across the country. With every speech, my thinking about gymnastics began to change. It's not that I didn't love the sport. I absolutely loved flipping around and obtaining new skills. I also loved to travel and perform well at competitions. But I no longer began to refer to myself as a gymnast. I saw myself as an author and motivational speaker who happened to do gymnastics. Before long, I found myself wanting to walk away from the sport.

To everyone else in the gymnastics community, I was crazy. In fact, many people told my parents they were crazy for even entertaining my thoughts! It got to the point in which I started to question my own decision. Was I really making a mistake?

In order to make sure I wasn't making an emotional decision, my mom told me to give it a couple of months. She told me if I still felt the same way two months from that point, then she would walk into the gym with me to tell my coach I was done with the sport. Two months later, I felt exactly the same way. My feelings weren't negative, and it wasn't the adversity that I'd faced that made me want to give up the sport. In fact, I'll take this time to tell you that adversity alone never means that you should give up going after your dream. Hard times are not a general sign that you are headed in the wrong direction. (Imagine if J.K. Rowling had given up after the 12th publisher told her no.) In my case, however, multiple situations compounded the adversity to give me a different outlook on my future gymnastics career.

Between the consistent, chronic pain, the injuries, and my newly found career as an author and young motivational speaker, I just felt this tugging on my heart of God leading me in a different direction. And to everyone out there who told my parents I was wasting my talent, it turns out my experience in gymnastics was not wasteful at all. My knowledge and personal understanding of high-level gymnastics became vital to my ability to direct the gymnastics facility that my mom and I currently own today.

I don't know what would have happened if I continued in my gymnastics career. But I can imagine that my body would not have been able to keep up with the physical demands. Somehow, I feel like I would have ended up taking the same path of motivating individuals around the world; it just would've been later in my life under different circumstances. But fortunately, I didn't waste time in that sense. When I knew God was leading me in a certain direction, I ran with it. And to this day, I will tell anyone that giving up gymnastics was one of the best decisions I've ever made. That one choice has allowed me to travel the world, inspiring many audiences. By giving my efforts to doing what I can to make this world a better place, I have been blessed to be able to do some amazing things, and I can only imagine what the Lord has in store for me.

When thinking about my life in terms of gymnastics, I often connect to other situations. There are so many times when we, as women, are so set on an end result that we don't allow God to truly work through us. Perhaps we want a relationship to work so badly that we refuse to see signs that he's not the best person for us long term. Meanwhile, our true knight in shining armor is right around the corner. Maybe we're holding on to an awful job so very tight, simply because we want the security. Even though we have a strong business plan, extraordinary collaborators, and consistent signs that our business would be super successful, we don't step out in faith. Maybe we are even fired from a job, spending countless hours crying about our loss, when God really only allowed that to happen to force us to step out on our own.

If you really think about it, some of God's greatest blessings are unanswered prayers. Sometimes when you think you are being rejected, you are really being redirected toward something better. You thought all hope was gone when you lost your job, without even realizing that the business you started out of necessity would continue to blossom in more ways than you could imagine. You thought your life was over when your husband left you, not understanding that God was bringing you a man who would help you grow beyond measure. You thought your child would never walk a positive path in life, not understanding that they would eventually use their journey to encourage other young people facing adversity. Remember this: Things will always be okay in the end. So, if things are not okay right now, then it's not the end. God is still working.

In everything that you do, pray about your decisions, and pay attention to signs. Don't hold on so tight to what *you* want that you fail to acknowledge what *He* wants for you. On a consistent basis, ask God to direct your mind and guide your reasoning. I'm a strong believer that God helps those who help themselves. In that regard, you can't just pray for prosperity without putting in the work. These seven practices are key for you to achieve the results you want in each area of your life. But your plans and God's plan must go hand in hand. As long as your actions are in alignment with God's will and purpose for your life, then no situation or human being can stop you. Once you truly believe that, you are well on your way!

"The steps of a good man are ordered by the Lord,
and He delights in his way." Psalm 37:23

Prosperous Points

- Push through adversity. Use your difficult circumstances to teach you, not defeat you. Continue pushing forward, despite the struggles you may be facing.
- Keep the big picture in mind. Don't lose sight of your goals. Remember this quote: "When you feel like giving up, remember why you held on so long in the first place."
- Stop trying to pray the adversity away. Without adversity, we would never know what we are truly capable of achieving. At the end of the day, pressure is what creates diamonds.
- Never cut what you can untie. Sometimes things get hard. Sometimes you will be tempted to give up. But you should never make a negative, permanent decision because of a temporary situation.
- Listen to God. It doesn't matter how badly we want something. If it is not in God's plan for us, it's not going to be sustainable.

Now, What?

Now that you understand these powerful seven practices of prosperous women, it's time to get to work! Don't let another day pass in which you are not closer to achieving prosperity in all aspects of your life. Your goals may be different from the goals of your sister, mother, daughter, aunt, niece, or best friend. And guess what? That is perfectly okay! Your journey will be different from anyone else's, and your successes won't be the same either. The most important thing is that you become the best version of yourself that you can be.

Whatever your desires may be, you know you want to be great! You didn't wake up this morning with the thought, "I just want to be mediocre." So, don't be! Start implementing the seven practices into your life today. Create a vision for your life, and meticulously work hard toward your dreams and goals. Through this hard work, don't forget the significance of mental strength, and learn to prioritize your time for both work and play. Remove yourself from negative people and situations whenever you're able. And when you experience failure, learn from it. Without a doubt, you will experience tough seasons, but you can never give up.

You may not be able to do every single thing in this book at once, but you can do something. I guarantee there are things you can do at this very moment for which your future self will thank you. Don't hesitate. Do those things. Each day is not promised, but the fact that you have breath in your body is a testament to the fact that God still has more for you to do. There is a purpose for your life. So make the most of it! Use each of these seven practices to achieve prosperity in each and every aspect of your life.

As I said before, these seven practices work together to create a formula for success. One or two practices don't achieve the same results as the combined effort of all seven. While it can take weeks, months, and even years to personally master the tasks of creating visions, working hard, developing mental strength, prioritizing, cutting off negativity, learning from failure, and never giving up, trust me on one thing: Taking the time to develop in each of these seven areas is totally worth it.

I wish you the best in all of your endeavors on your journey to becoming the best version of yourself. Remember that as long as your goals are in alignment with God's will, nothing and no one can stop you. Now, go prosper!

ACKNOWLEDGEMENTS

Each and every one of my life experiences, no matter how big or small, has contributed in some way to the formation of this book. For that, I thank the Lord above. Although I could never understand or fully appreciate the ways in which He works, I do believe that all things work together for good. Everything that I have gone through has helped me develop in various areas of my life. Without these experiences, I know that I would not be able to convincingly write and speak about these life-changing seven practices.

Though writing this book has been extremely rewarding, it was oftentimes a lonely process. Hours were spent locked away in my room with just my computer to keep me company. During this time, I was especially appreciative of my immediate family. My mom, dad, brother, and husband have been a consistent source of love and encouragement for me. I am forever grateful for all of their support of my numerous endeavors over the years. Because of them, I am inspired to be the absolute best woman that I can be.

Although my immediate family has been crucial in

providing day-to-day support of this book's publication, I give a multitude of thanks to my extended family and close friends as well. Their never-ending love has uplifted me in ways that I cannot even begin to explain.

Without a doubt, I appreciate anyone and everyone who has given me advice and/or reassurance on my journey to this point. I never underestimate the value of a kind word, simply because the amazing kindness of others has helped to open many doors in my own life. I am also thankful to anyone who has ever tried to hold me back or put me down. That negativity allowed me the distinct opportunity to stand back and see God work. What I've realized is that we each have our own path, and I am extremely appreciative of that. As women, there is no reason for us to tear each other down. Instead, we should help build each other up. And that is a gift I am excited to give others. Thank you!

Raven Magwood is a sought-after motivational speaker, author, and filmmaker who has dedicated her young life to one thing: inspiring people around the world to become the best versions of themselves. Since giving her first speech at only 12 years old, Raven has travelled internationally, providing individuals with the tools they need to unlock their full potential. Described by many as an achievement expert, she has worked with hundreds of thousands of students, educators, CEOs, business leaders, youth activists, pastors, and many more! Although Raven stays very busy, she enjoys spending time with family and friends. When she's not writing, speaking, coaching, or shooting a film, Raven enjoys shopping, volunteering at church, listening to music, and traveling. For more information about Raven, please visit www.RavenMagwood.com.

CPSIA information can be obtained
at www.ICGtesting.com
Printed in the USA
LVHW111034141119
636906LV00002B/1/P

9 781977 208828